THE FILMS OF
S T E V E N
SPIELBERG

THE FILMS OF

STEVEN

SPIELBERG

NEIL SINYARD

HAMLYN

Published by
The Hamlyn Publishing Group Limited
a division of the Octopus Group PLC,
Michelin House, 81 Fulham Road,
London SW3 6RB.
and distributed for them by
Octopus Distribution Services Limited,
Rushden, Northamptonshire NN10 9RZ.

Copyright © 1987 Bison Books Ltd.

Produced by
Bison Books Ltd.
176 Old Brompton Road,
London SW5,
England.

ISBN 0-600-55226-8

Printed in Hong Kong

Second impression 1987
Third impression 1988

Page 1: Steven Spielberg, in his E.T. hat, lines up a shot for his next mega-hit, *Indiana Jones and the Temple of Doom*.

Pages 2-3: A typical child's view of the adult world in Spielberg: Elliott (Henry Thomas) watches the search for the alien in *E.T. – The Extra-Terrestrial*.

Pages 4-5: A good example of mysterious lighting in Spielberg. The mother and the medium unite to fight the forces from the other side in *Poltergeist*.

CONTENTS

INTRODUCTION

To borrow a phrase, the force is with Steven Spielberg. Almost everything he touches turns to gold. He is currently in a position of such commercial power that Hollywood needs him much more than he needs it – a position that most probably provokes a residual resentment on the part of rivals and dependants. To add insult to envy, Spielberg has youth on his side: he is not yet 40 years old.

Yet Spielberg seems to have attained such eminence relatively painlessly, and through a film personality that has touched superstardom by being attractive rather than abrasive and likeable rather than lewd. The impression one has of Spielberg from his films is that he combines a disarming blend of innocence with precociousness. The sense of innocence comes from the childlike wonder with which he imbues such colossal hits as *Close Encounters of the Third Kind* (1977) and *E.T. – The Extra-Terrestrial* (1982). Their success is probably attributable to the way Spielberg convinces us that the humanity and sentiment are completely sincere. He has the soul of a Walt Disney, the heart of a Peter Pan – he is not called wunderkind for nothing. The sense of precociousness comes from the technique, the kind of sophisticated craftsmanship where camera placement seems instinctively right and the ability to tell a story through the camera comes as natural as breathing. In this respect, Spielberg recalls Hitchcock, as he does also in his insistence on the emotional rather than intellectual power of film and the responsibility of the filmmaker to fill the screen with imagery so exciting that it transports the audience out of their normal lives. All this is a partial explanation for the breadth of Spielberg's appeal. It touches the film fan and the film buff, the adven-

Left: Steven Spielberg and his extra-terrestrial friend, created by Carlo Rambaldi.

Right: The light at the end of the road – a haunting image that prepares us for the advent of something extraordinary in *Close Encounters of the Third Kind*.

turer in every child and the child in every adult. He is an escapist artist.

Spielberg rose to prominence with the extremely talented generation of 'movie brats' (Francis Coppola, Martin Scorsese, John Milius, Brian de Palma, George Lucas, Paul Schrader, and others) who took over Hollywood in the early 1970s. However, he is very different in many respects from most of them. He tells stories rather than dissects characters or indulges his style. He believes in the filmmaker as entertainer more than in the director as *auteur*, or ego. According to Spielberg, cinema is the place for the eliciting of mass emotion, not the expression of private pain.

Nevertheless, although he has been quite happy to be labelled a 'popcorn entertainment' filmmaker, he has deftly shuffled some subtlety and sophistication into that populist label. It would be wrong to identify him exclusively with the cinema of spectacle and special effects. He is good with actors and superb with children, and is very careful to give his movies sufficient humanity for an audience to identify with the person who is having the experience. He has described his style and his film world as 'heightened reality' but it is a reality that is fun to live rather than depressing or pessimistic or intolerable.

What are the movies like, and what are they about? They are about heroes but they are neither sanctimonious nor too serious about heroism. Very often they satirize the macho male, who is variously chewed over, parodied and upstaged by the meek. They are about the media, and cast an intelligent and often ironical eye over their operation. They have a seductive charm and sensitivity, which comes partly from Spielberg's gift of entering into the world of children. This contrasts with his seeming disinclination to enter the world of adult anxiety, whether it be social, psychological or sexual. There are considerable tensions in Spielberg's films, as anyone who has jumped and shivered and sweated his way through *Duel* (1971), *Something Evil* (1972) and *Jaws* (1975) knows. But the tensions in Spielberg correspond more to the frisson of the cartoon and the funfair than the permanent pains of real life. Indeed, as *Close Encounters of the Third Kind* and *E.T. – The Extra-Terrestrial* intriguingly demonstrate, Spielberg can make the most thrilling and suspenseful films without any reference at all to the presence of evil, or even badness.

The basic pattern of a Spielberg movie is the situation of ordinary people being compelled to react to extraordinary events. The movies invariably begin with a world close enough to our

own to forge some identification. This permits Spielberg to reveal his particular gifts as a shrewd and sardonic observer of suburban style and to establish characters who will be, as he puts it, our 'human guides through the world of mechanized madness.' Having established that world, the movies then move logically but audaciously toward ultimate extravagant adventure, offering not an analysis of modern life but an escape into purest fantasy.

Escape is perhaps the most recurrent situation in a Spielberg film and a dominant theme. It raises several questions about the meaning of the films. If the characters seek escape, is what they are escaping *to* more or less significant than what they are escaping *from*? (This is a key question of *Close Encounters*.) Should one regard the escape as a liberation from life's problems or as an evasion of them? (An important question in *Jaws* and even Spielberg's 1985 production, *The Goonies*.) Might one see the role of the cinema in Spielberg's own life as a form of ultimate escape – from the reality of

an unhappy childhood and from, as he has acknowledged himself, the necessity of having to grow up?

Whatever the implications of the theme, it is clear that audiences are drawn to Spielberg's movies for precisely the sense of escape that they offer – from the drabness of ordinary life, from personal problems, from the limitations of reality or from the boredom of television. For many people such escapism has always been the essence of the appeal of the cinema, which, in their terms, should provide fantasy not fact, magic not morbidity. By bringing innocence and excitement back into the cinema more effectively than anyone since Walt Disney, Spielberg has brought mass audiences back into them as well, and on a scale that the industry thought it had lost forever.

It is interesting that there is no critical concensus about what is Spielberg's best film to date. He himself would probably favor *E.T.*, for its quality of wonder, but one could make equally strong claims for the supreme suspense of *Jaws* or the emotional uplift

of *Close Encounters*. Some critics have gone on record as preferring the tragicomedy of *Sugarland Express* (1974) and even the firecracker farce of *1941*. One can draw two implications from this: that Spielberg's work displays more variety and versatility than he is given credit for, which is the reason that individual critics respond to different things in his work; and that his ultimate masterpiece is yet to come, which is a mouth-watering prospect. For the present, this book invites the reader to ponder afresh his or her favorite Spielberg, and savor some of the most imaginative and popular moments of recent movie history.

Right: A dangerous moment for Short Round (Ke Huy Quan) in *Indiana Jones and the Temple of Doom*, a 'prequel' to the massively successful *Raiders of the Lost Ark*.

Below: Spielberg is in the center of this production shot from *Jaws*. Despite the relaxed pose filming was extremely arduous and Spielberg was afraid the technicians were planning to drown him in revenge.

FROM HOME MOVIES TO HOLLYWOOD

Steven Spielberg's films are personal without being autobiographical. Although the incidents in his movies rarely derive from direct recollection, since he led quite a sheltered life ('I'd never been robbed, been in a fight, seen a corpse, and never eaten Italian food until I came to New York'), the feelings in his movies can partially be traced to aspects of his upbringing. The significant aspects of this are the suburban lifestyle of his childhood to which he both reacted and drew sustenance; and the separation of his father, an electrical engineer, and his mother, a classical pianist, when he was in his teens. Spielberg's characterization of the family in his films seems to have been influenced by that event, as we shall see.

Spielberg was born in Cincinnati, Ohio, on 18 December 1947. The place (Spielberg hates being called the 'Cincinnati Kid' and anyway was mainly brought up in Phoenix, Arizona) is less significant than the date – the year, as Spielberg said, that the word 'flying saucer' was first used. He has said that he inherited his fascination with science fiction from his father, and that his similar obsession with a camera from an early age derived from his father's photographic incompetence. Interestingly, Spielberg seems to have been a filmmaker almost before he became a film fan. Significantly, the films that most stuck in his mind as a child were those of Disney – crying at *Bambi* and *Dumbo* and having nightmares for a week after the 'Night on Bare Mountain' sequence in *Fantasia* (perhaps part of the inspiration for the mountain imagery in *Close Encounters*). But he was more interested in filmmaking at that time than film history.

He had made his first film by the age of 12, an 8mm account of a stagecoach robbery lasting 3½ minutes and costing 10 dollars. A year later he made a 40-minute war movie on 8mm entitled *Escape to Nowhere*. At the age of 16 he made his most ambitious teenage project, *Firelight*, a 140-minute epic about UFOs which is clearly the forerunner of *Close Encounters of the Third Kind*.

Unlike a number of his contemporaries, however, men such as Francis Coppola, George Lucas and John Milius, Spielberg's entry into the film industry was not via film school, for his school grades were not good enough to ensure acceptance. In fact, according to legend, which Spielberg has neither authoritatively confirmed nor denied, his entry seems to have been literally through Universal's front gate. Wearing a suit and tie and carrying a briefcase, he would walk past the doorman, who for months thought he was the son of the head of the studio, and settle in

Left: Old and new Hollywood come face to face. Spielberg's first directing assignment is an episode from the television series, *Night Gallery*, called 'Eyes,' starring the formidable Joan Crawford.

Right: Spielberg prepares to create orderly panic in *Jaws*.

had to endure the antagonism of hardened veteran technicians who would joke about having to interrupt work for the director's 'milk and cookies break,' and was thrown into the deep end immediately by having to direct an episode of Rod Serling's TV series *Night Gallery* starring the formidable Joan Crawford.

Writers Richard Levinson and William Link recall that Spielberg at this time would ask them to come down to the set because nobody would talk to him. He had directed a script of theirs, *Murder by the Book* (1971), for the TV series *Columbo* starring Peter Falk as the rumpled police inspector, and they had been tremendously impressed by the assurance of the crosscutting, the handling of the suspense and the lively eye for detail. Later they would be even more impressed by his direction of another script of theirs, the television movie *Savage* (1973), a pilot for a series about an investigative reporter (Martin Landau) that never materialized. The characters and plotting are uninteresting, but the technique is extremely audacious, the cameras running riot in a TV studio set is an indication of Spielberg's early fascination with the mechanics of the media. 'Our script was awful,' said Link, 'but Steve's work was dazzling, electrifying..... He took all sorts of chances. He'd do a five-page

Left: On the set of *Something Evil*, a brilliant TV horror movie first broadcast by CBS in January 1972.

Below: *Duel*, Spielberg's made-for-TV movie became an instant classic and was released as a feature film in Europe.

one of the numerous vacant offices waiting for something to happen. All that happened was a bit of tutorship in the editing room and the experience of being thrown off the set of Hitchcock's *Torn Curtain*.

Spielberg's break came when producer Dennis Hoffman arranged for him to make a 20-minute short, *Amblin'*, which fared well at the Atlanta Film Festival and was photographed, incidentally, by Allen Daviau, a friend who was later to be his cameraman on *E.T.* On the basis of *Amblin'*, he was employed by Universal executive Sidney Scheinberg on a seven-year contract in 1969, at the tender age of 21. It has never been easy to be a boy wonder in Hollywood, as Orson Welles had found, and the late 1960s was a particularly sensitive time. The industry was discovering that a lot of the young directors it had hired on the strength of the runaway success of *Easy Rider* (1968) had only youth and not talent to recommend them. Spielberg

The killer's weapon a 40-ton truck!

DUEL AA

Starring DENNIS WEAVER Screenplay by RICHARD MATHESON · Based on his published story · Directed by STEVEN SPIELBERG · Produced by GEORGE ECKSTEIN · A UNIVERSAL PICTURE ■ TECHNICOLOR®

Above: Our first mirror view of the driver in *Duel*. Mann (Dennis Weaver) sets off on a journey which will bring him to the brink of breakdown.

scene in one-take, choreographing the people and the camera.' Levinson, who was to become a director himself (*Diner, The Natural*) and to work in that capacity on the Spielberg production *The Young Sherlock Holmes* (1986), found even more to admire in an episode

Spielberg did for a series called *The Psychiatrist*, in which Clu Gulager plays a golfer dying of cancer. Levinson recalled it as remarkably acted, as grim as hell, and all this from 'the kid they said didn't know people.' Spielberg has intimated he thought this episode represented the best of his television work, but his talent was to be overwhelmingly confirmed by two TV films, which still rank among the best movies ever made

for television – *Duel* (1971) and *Something Evil* (1972).

Based on a Richard Matheson story and shot in 16 days, *Duel* tells the story of a timid suburban male, David Mann (Dennis Weaver), who is menaced on the highway by the motiveless malignancy of a truck whose driver we are never allowed to see. At first the truck seems merely to be playing a game, jokily preventing Mann from overtaking and hence reaching his important business meeting in time. Things become more serious when the truckdriver beckons Mann to pass and the hero is almost guided into the path of a passing car. On another occasion Mann is attacked by the truck in a phone booth in a Snakerama, which seems to unleash all the creatures of hell out of Mann's imagination (giant tarantulas and wriggling snakes will similarly menace Indiana Jones in *Raiders of the Lost Ark*). He is finally forced into a joust-like confrontation, the two vehicles charging toward each other like medieval knights in armor, with Mann at the last moment jumping to safety.

Part of the effectiveness of *Duel* is that the spareness of its structure

Below: The truck runs amok in the snakerama in *Duel*.

Above: More highway madness in *Duel*, as once again the malevolent truck makes its presence felt.

allows for wide-ranging implications and interpretation. It could be read, firstly, as a portrait in paranoia. During a confrontation with a driver in a cafe, Mann is told that 'you need help,' and one could see the cacophonous contest that develops between Mann and the truck as an externalization of the hero's inward insecurity and incipient nervous breakdown. It is also an allegory of the war between man and machine, with the car as man's enemy and prison, a trap from which he must spring himself. The hero's lifestyle seems as regimented as that of the truck until this adventure drives him into a completely different path of behavior. *Duel* can also be seen as an allegory about American pressure and aggression, and what has happened to the old frontier spirit now that the horse has been displaced by the car.

The hero of *Duel*, said Spielberg, 'is typical of that lower middle-class American who's insulated by suburban modernization. A man like that never expects to be challenged by anything more than his television set breaking down and having to call the repair man.' The opening scenes play wittily with a subtheme of emasculation, as a man on the hero's car radio insists that he might be the man of the family but he is not the *head* of the family. This theme is continued when Mann, mistakenly, refuses to have his radiator hose repaired and, to the pump attendant's comment 'You're the boss' replies 'Not in my house I'm not.' When he phones home, we learn that his wife has been sexually harassed at a party the previous evening and he has done nothing about it. In

the cafe, the hero is plainly intimidated by the redneck machismo of the truck drivers. Step-by-step, the film will drive Mann into a situation where he must assert himself for his own survival. Spielberg clinches this in a wonderful image: Mann clicks on his seat belt in defiant determination, like a Westerner fastening his holster in readiness for the final shootout. His name becomes symbolic. David takes on Goliath, and becomes a man.

On the other hand, it is possible to ignore all these signals of symbolism and simply take *Duel* as, in all senses, a remarkable suspense vehicle, in which the truck is simply there to generate tense and exciting situations. As an exercise in suspense, Spielberg's direction is worthy of comparison with Hitchcock. It has something of Hitchcock's sense of humor, as in the revelation that the truck might hate Mann but it likes children, and can move a school bus when Mann himself has, significantly, not got sufficient push. The nightmare in broad daylight recalls the famous crop-duster assault in Hitchcock's *North by Northwest*; the tense car drive and use of recriminatory self-tormenting monologue reminds one of *Psycho*; the suggestion of malign intelligence in the strategy of the truck's attacks is similar to the way Hitchcock generates suspense in *The Birds*. There are many tremendous moments: the lights of the truck gleaming at the base of the tunnel like demon's eyes; a judicious comic long shot which makes the chase look like that of a Disneyesque black beetle in pursuit of a red ant; Mann's sleep next

Right: The truck and the driver (Dennis Weaver) about to lock horns again in *Duel*.

to a car graveyard which, even at a point of respite, is a reminder that there is a vehicle out there wanting him dead.

In retrospect one can see a number of future Spielberg themes in *Duel*. The situation of highway pursuit will be continued in *The Sugarland Express*, and there is an anticipation of *Jaws* in the antics of a supernatural beast attempting to devour a hero who must respond physically to the challenge. There is also a shadowy class theme in *Duel*, where an unmistakably proletarian truck menaces a genteel, middleclass vehicle, as if determined to challenge and annihilate the complacency and values that that kind of materialistic middle-class possession signifies. This not only anticipates a dimension of the class tensions in *Sugarland Express* and *Jaws*, but also an important theme of forthcoming anarchic American horror movies like *Race with the Devil*

Left: An image of modern man as caged, wary and afraid. Dennis Weaver's performance in *Duel* is a brilliant study in rising hysteria.

Below left: The truck crashes down a cliff like a fatally wounded beast in the finale to *Duel*.

Below: The final confrontation in *Duel*. In a gripping climax, the hero will finally jump clear from his car.

(1975) and *The Hills Have Eyes* (1977).

Spielberg's TV horror movie, *Something Evil* (1972), on the face of it, looks quite conventional. A New York family buy a house in the country only to discover that the farmhouse is haunted by an evil spirit. Robert Clouse's exciting, unpretentious script is filled out with some witty detail. The husband (Darren McGavin) is a director of television commercials, which allows for a satire on the seriousness with which advertising jingles are constructed, as well as providing a blood-chilling moment when the husband inspects the film he has taken at his house and notices two malevolent eyes gleaming through the front window. Johnny Whittaker plays Stevie, a boy in danger of demonic possession. In scenes where Stevie frightens his sister with a toy spider and is in turn terrified by his mother, who is either possessive or possessed, one is reminded of a classic thriller like Jack Clayton's *The Innocents* (1961), the film version of Henry James' *Turn of the Screw*. As the mother who has to fight evil and personal breakdown in her singlehanded attempt to save her son, Sandy Dennis gives a performance of neurotic intensity that is both touching and terrifying.

Spielberg's direction is nothing short of magnificent. There are splendid montages as mother paints and creates models and mobiles that will eventually be significant in resisting the evil spells; dazzling dissolves and sinister camera placement for stealthy, apprehensive entrances into fearful places; and again a Hitchcockian sense of the moment to throw away explanatory dialogue (the explanation of the house's past) when it is less interesting than the mystery and the menace. Again, in retrospect, one notices aspects of the film which will become characteristic of Spielberg: the warmth of the domestic scenes and the excellence of the children's performances; the situation of city people out of their milieu; and, particularly, the active role of the resourceful mother taking the place of an ineffectual or absent father. In *Something Evil*, as in future Spielberg films, the mother/son relationship is very important, and the gripping finale, in which the mother clings to her son's body and soul within the magic circle against the power of demonic possession, is an extraordinarily suspenseful rather than sentimental vindication of maternal love.

Despite the enormous impact made by *Duel* and *Something Evil* when they

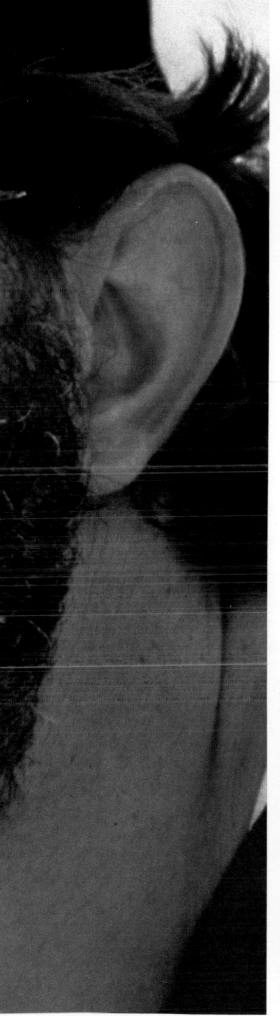

Above: Spielberg directs an outdoor scene from *Something Evil*. Seated at the easel is Sandy Dennis, who plays the first of Spielberg's resourceful, courageous mother figures who will risk themselves for their children.

were transmitted on American television – in November 1971 and January 1972 respectively – Spielberg still had to wait before his own big-screen opportunity arrived. Yet there were a number of portents that suggested it would only be a matter of time. He wrote the story for a Cliff Robertson movie about barnstorming pilots, *Ace Eli and Rodger of the Skies* (1973), which never got off the ground. He spent months of preparation on the Burt Reynolds' movie, *White Lightning*, but

withdrew when he assessed that overall control would rest with the star and not with the director. In 1973 *Duel* was boosted to feature-length and released as a movie in Europe to great acclaim and success. It was no surprise, then, that his official feature-film debut should prove to be exceptional – indeed, in the words of the influential critic of *The New Yorker*, Pauline Kael, it was 'one of the most phenomenal debut films in the history of movies.'

Left: Friend, producer and fellow movie brat, George Lucas, maker of *Star Wars*.

Below: Spielberg (right) rehearses Sandy Dennis and Johnny Whittaker in *Something Evil*.

THE SUGARLAND EXPRESS

*T*he Sugarland Express was based on an actual incident that had occurred in Texas in 1969, though the events and the characters are reshaped by Spielberg and his first-time screenwriters, Hal Barwood and Matthew Robbins (old friends of Spielberg who will crop up again to play the two missing airmen who step out of the Mother Ship at the end of *Close Encounters*). Lou Jean Poplin (Goldie Hawn) springs her husband Clovis (William Atherton) from a Pre-Release Center in order to regain custody of their son, who has been taken from them because of their unfitness as parents and entrusted to foster parents in Sugarland. In one sense, their extreme behavior will justify this judgment of their parental ability. In another, the lengths to which they go in order to reclaim their child will testify to the depth of their love.

On the way, they take as hostage a young policeman, Maxwell Slide (Michael Sacks). This facilitates their passage to Sugarland but it also ensures a posse of police in pursuit and a violent reception when they arrive at their destination. However, not only the police are in tow. 'Who else is out there?' queries Captain Tanner (Ben Johnson), the man in charge of the police operation who becomes aware that other forces are interested and involved. The answer is, firstly, the media, who see the opportunity to fill out a lively story and bestow upon the couple a disproportionate notoriety. Also taking a keen interest are the general public, to whom Lou Jean and Clovis become instant celebrities, like Bonnie and Clyde.

Right: On the way to becoming a (short lived) legend. Goldie Hawn plays Lou Jean Poplin in *The Sugarland Express.*

Below: Publicity had trouble in expressing the spirit of *Sugarland Express*, perhaps the reason it was a commercial failure.

Winner of Best Screenplay Cannes Film Festival 1974

The true story of a girl who took on all of Texas and almost won.

A Zanuck / Brown Production
GOLDIE HAWN in
THE SUGARLAND EXPRESS AA

Co-starring **Ben Johnson**, Michael Sacks, William Atherton
Music by John Williams Screenplay by Hal Barwood & Matthew Robbins
Story by Steven Spielberg and Hal Barwood & Matthew Robbins
Directed by Steven Spielberg Produced by Richard D. Zanuck and David Brown
A Universal Picture Technicolor® Panavision® Distributed by Cinema International Corporation.

Oscar Wilde once commented that 'Americans are great hero-worshippers and they always take their heroes from the criminal classes. I, myself, would say that America was not discovered, it was merely detected.' The negative side to that is the possibility of overreaction by the forces of law and order, anxious to save face and stamp down on any romanticizing of the lawbreaker. Things start to develop in the way that Captain Tanner most fears: a minor felony will, stage-by-stage, build into a crisis he can no longer control.

'I've discovered I've got this preoccupation with ordinary people pursued by large forces,' said Spielberg, who might have been remembering *Duel* and *Something Evil* and was certainly anticipating *Close Encounters*. The large forces in this case are the Texas police force whose gathering exasperation and humiliation are pushing them toward an extreme solution. As in *Duel*, Spielberg makes strange, fearful and funny patterns out of the behavior of cars, and the frenzied pursuit and slapstick collisions often evoke the *Road-Runner* cartoons which Spielberg loved. But within the linear development of plot is a wide variety of mood, eloquently expanded by photography from Vilmos Zsigmond that alternates between realism and lyricism. Spielberg crosscuts between farce and

intimations of impending doom, so that the pranks of the Poplins, the mania of the media, and the deadly preparations of the police marksmen jostle together in tense alignment. The range of mood is superbly encapsulated in a scene where Lou Jean and Clovis are hiding in a trailer near a drive-in cinema and, for entertainment, improvise their own soundtrack noises to the movie cartoon they can see but not hear. Suddenly the zany action yet insistent violence of the cartoon seems to strike a responsive chord in Clovis, whose expression (an eloquent piece of acting by Atherton) changes from hilarity to creeping apprehension.

Kidding you along for some time with its joky tone and some sharp comedy cameos (Spielberg has a particularly impressive line-up of crotchety old folk), *Sugarland Express* suddenly confronts you with the desperate seriousness of the situation. As in Arthur Penn's *Bonnie and Clyde* (1967), hillbilly comedy is suddenly escalating toward tragedy, and a picaresque pastoral is turning paranoid. Shortly after the cartoon sequence, the fugitives are fired on by right-wing vigilantes and, although they escape, a single image of a child in a state of shock after the shooting shows that the tone has now shifted decisively to one of foreboding. From here, Spielberg turns on the tension. The final

sequence is close to agonizing, as Clovis is shot, Slide tries desperately to mop up his injuries, Lou Jean becomes hysterical, the car lurches woundedly out of control, and the trophies of their journey – rifle, baby boots, a teddy bear – are thrown out of the car window to signal the final death-throes of their enterprise.

Because of his later association with special effects, Spielberg has often been underrated as a director of actors, but the leading performances in *Sugarland Express* have a real sensitivity and style in what are all quite tricky assignments. Goldie Hawn has yet to surpass her performance as Lou Jean, aligning her usual coy winsomeness with a tough determination and a neurotic edge that makes the character both complex and disturbing. 'She was the villain, the real heavy,' said Spielberg of this character and he amplifies this with a camera

Above right: Clovis acquires firearms along the way to reclaim his infant son and sinks deeper into trouble.

Below right: The infectious grin of Lou Jean conceals an impetuous nature and a dangerous determination.

Below: A snatched moment of happiness for husband Clovis Poplin (William Atherton) and wife Lou Jean (Goldie Hawn) in *The Sugarland Express*.

style that seems to watch and follow the lady quite edgily and often stands surprised at her next move. It is Lou Jean who initiates all the significant events – the decision to escape, to kidnap the cop, to push Clovis out to the house to claim the child. Her tragic flaw is presented as an inability to wait: for her husband's release, for sex, for a pee, and, crucially, for her son. William Atherton as Clovis and Michael Sacks as Slide are equally fine in more muted roles, basically sensitive types who find something to admire in each other. 'It's two men who really began in the same small town and went different ways,' Spielberg said. 'One took the road to law and order, the other took a wrong turn in life.' As Captain Tanner, who has avoided killing anyone in his police career and who has developed an affection for the two runaways, Ben Johnson exudes a quiet authority that is more sympathetic than his Oscar-winning role in *The Last Picture Show* (1972).

Like *Duel, Sugarland Express* is a road movie-cum-western that examines something of the legacy of America's gun culture. Like the earlier TV movie, *Savage*, it is fascinated by the operations of the media and particularly by the paradox whereby the increasing sophistication of communication technology seems only to result in a decreasing effectiveness of human communication. Like *Something Evil*, it is a film about a mother's love. There is also the class subtheme that was implied in *Duel*. The child has been taken away from its wild lower-class parents and put into a home with impeccably middle-class credentials. This foster home is transformed into a fortress as the anarchic vehicle of Lou Jean and Clovis draws nearer. Two neat details particularly underline the class theme and the tension between these two

Right: Captain Tanner (Ben Johnson) prepares for a showdown in *The Sugarland Express*. Despite his menacing appearance here, he is sympathetic to the fugitives.

Below: Almost an entire state's police force chase after the Poplins.

N 2 772

worlds: the moment when the foster mother (Louise Latham) notices the armed policemen come into her house and her first thought is to move a precious vase out of the hall; and the foster father's reaction, when he assesses what the police are doing and simply says: 'Officer, I know you're not gonna let me shoot the son-of-a-bitch, but at least you can use my rifle. . . .'

Left: Clovis takes evasive action from vigilantes in a used car lot.

Below: The hostage P C Slide (Michael Sacks) is trapped in the crossfire when the Poplins become targets for gun-happy Texans.

By any criterion, *Sugarland Express* is a stunning directorial debut, a technical *tour de force* that also demonstrates a gift for comedy and a rapport with young actors. A melancholy footnote, however, is that it was not a commercial success. Various reasons have been put forward to explain this. For one thing, its release was delayed by Universal in order to capitalize on a Christmas release for its big new film, *The Sting* (1973). When it was released later, not only had favorable word-of-mouth gone a little stale, but also *Sugarland* was sandwiched between two films with very similar subjects – Robert Altman's *Thieves Like Us* (1973) and Terrence Malick's *Badlands* (1974). Also *Sugarland* turned out to be an

Above: The two fugitives and their hostage on their way to Sugarland, in a car now ominously riddled with bullet-holes.

Right: A moment of relaxation on set. Goldie Hawn chats with the co-producer Richard Zanuck, whose son Harrison plays the part of Baby Langston.

extremely difficult film to sell. 'We all realized we were in trouble when we had so much trouble coming up with an ad campaign,' said the film's producer, Richard Zanuck. 'We couldn't get any one visual idea that would express what the picture was.'

The main difficulty seems to have been with the off-beat and abrasive

characterization of the outlaw couple. Audiences seemed split both ways, some finding them too plebeian and raucous for easy sympathy, others finding them likeable but, as a consequence, also finding the tragic ending too painful. It is a film that bubbles with life, but there is a brutality beneath its innocence and it hurts. There are those who particularly lament the commercial failure of *Sugarland* because they feel that, in terms of boldness of characterization and tone, Spielberg has done nothing finer and might since have been tempted to play a little safe. By one of those curious little ironies that seem part and parcel of the film industry Spielberg was told that *Sugarland* was doing disastrous box-office business on the very first day of shooting of the film which was to become one of the most colossal financial successes in movie history – *Jaws*.

Below: Spielberg, with cameraman Vilmos Zsigmond, on location.

DOZU..
USE OF REAL
LIVE
FOOTAGE OF
SHARKS—
SCARY STILL

At first, Spielberg was doubtful about whether to accept the *Jaws* assignment. He thought that the situation of shark-menaces-humans might seem too similar to that of truck-terrifies-man in *Duel*. He was encouraged when a cast was assembled that he liked: Robert Shaw rather than Sterling Hayden as the he-man Quint; Roy Scheider rather than Charlton Heston

Left: Brody leans anxiously over his son, who has nearly become the next course on the shark's menu.

Below: The first shark attack. We do not see the shark itself at this stage, but its terrifying power is implied through the terror of its victim (Susan Backlinie).

as the police chief Brody; and, as the ocean expert Hooper, a young actor, Richard Dreyfuss, who had impressed Spielberg greatly in the hit film of his friend, George Lucas, *American Graffiti* (1973).

Having accepted the challenge, Spielberg then found that the actual shooting of the film was a complete nightmare. The original shooting schedule of 52 days was tripled because of the complications of filming at sea, with the result that the picture went grossly over budget. In the 12-hour day that the crew was working on *Jaws*, Spielberg calculated that only four were concerned with the actual filming. The rest consisted in anchoring the boats, fighting the waves and struggling with the mechanical shark. Richard Dreyfuss recalls that he thought the film

might well turn out to be the flop of the year because everything hinged not on how well he and the others acted but on how well the shark acted. The shark's early screen tests were not very promising.

Although some documentary footage was to be interpolated, it was obviously not going to be possible to film *Jaws* with a real shark, and the construction of a mechanical model (fondly nicknamed 'Bruce') created massive problems. It was made of polyurethane, was 24 feet long and weighed 1½ tons. On its first test it sank, and on its second it exploded. An early inspection of the rushes revealed that the shark was cross-eyed and that its jaws would not shut.

The problems compelled Spielberg to be more inventive and to conceal the

Above: The bathers rush for the beach as the shark strikes again in *Jaws*.

Right: Filming aboard the Orca in *Jaws*. Spielberg said 'the whole idea of being on somebody else's menu was just utterly horrifying.'

Below: Brody (Roy Scheider, center) and Hooper (Richard Dreyfuss, right) try to convince the Mayor (Murray Hamilton) of the shark menace.

shark for as long as possible in the movie. Its presence is suggested by twisting underwater camerawork and by the hungry groans and mechanical, insistent, Stravinskian rhythms of John Williams's remarkable score. (It might be worth recalling that Stravinsky's *The Rite of Spring* was used by Disney to evoke prehistoric monsters in *Fantasia*, and this may well have had an influence on the sound of fear that Williams created.) By such means, the horror of the shark is transferred into the imagination of the audience. The strategy is rather like that of Henry James in his classic ghost story, *The Turn of the Screw*. 'Only make the reader's general vision of evil intense enough,' explained James in his preface, 'and his own experience, his own imagination, his own sympathy and horror will supply him quite sufficiently with all the particulars. Make him *think* the evil, make him think it for himself, and you are released from weak specifications.' Coincidentally perhaps, one of the most sinister characters in the James' story is also called Quint.

The story is simplicity itself. A shark is menacing the beach of Amity, literally killing off the tourist trade, and the search is on for the Great White Male to teach it that eating people is wrong. The first half of the film is a deft combination of Watergate and Ibsen's play, *An Enemy of the People*. It shows not only the shark threat but also the attempt of the Mayor (Murray Hamilton) and some of the townspeople to cover up the crisis in order not to frighten away the tourists. Is Amity as greedy as the shark? 'Amity is a summer town,' says the Mayor, 'we need summer dollars.' He embodies all the evil of modern commercial enterprises that put profit

Above: Roy Scheider discusses his role in *Jaws* with Peter Benchley (center), author of the novel, and Carl Gottlieb (right), who co-authored the screenplay with Benchley.

Below: Three men in a boat in *Jaws*, with the shark now in their sights.

Right: Robert Shaw plays Quint, an experienced seaman with his own score to settle with the shark, in *Jaws*.

before people. In a witty costuming detail, even the jackets that the Mayor wears are a kind of subliminal commercial for the beach: anchors on one, a kind of deck-chair design on another. The second half is pure sub-Hemingway as three men in a boat set out to kill the shark – Quint, a crusty old man of the sea, Hooper, young whiz-kid of the ocean, and Brody, a New Yorker cop who is almost literally out of his depth.

Peter Benchley, on whose novel the film is based, is credited as co-author of the screenplay with Carl Gottlieb (both of whom get to make an appearance in the film). As is often the case, however, the credits tell only half the story. Spielberg and his producers, Richard Zanuck and David Brown, worked hard on hammering out a screen story, making a number of significant changes to the novel (deleting Hooper's affair with Brody's wife, displacing the class conflict between Brody and the community onto Hooper and Quint, and allowing Hooper to survive.) Howard Sackler, author of the Pulitzer Prize-winning play *The Great White Hope*, was brought in to bolster the screenplay with his fishing expertise. Quint's long monologue about the sinking of the *Indianapolis* and the shark attack on the crew was written by John Milius. *Jaws* is a collaborative triumph and, in addition to the writers, actors and composer cited earlier, one might also pay tribute to the brilliantly controlled rhythms of Verna Field's editing. But

*became films in which
the Suspence is the
Duck of the Storylines.
In order make viewing
not as intence for the
audeences be implicated
humor.*

terms by the islanders, but is gradually vindicated by a slow slippage of menacing imagery – a disappearing dog, an anxious mother and a sudden, gushing fountain of red that signals a fatal attack. The moment when the victim in the underwater wreck bobs in front of Hooper's vision is a sizeable quick shock. Funnier and more frightening still is the shark's first appearance as Brody is nonchalantly tossing the bait into the water – a moment when the monster literally rises to the bait, pops up to say hello, and fills the frame as the embodiment of fear writ large.

There is a lot of humor in *Jaws*. Like Hitchcock, Spielberg knows its value in simultaneously winning over an audience but keeping them off their guard. Children play with a Killer Shark game in the amusement arcade. Brody's wife (Lorraine Gary) frets over whether she has packed the right things for her husband, as if he is off to spend two nights in a hotel rather than risk being on a killer shark's menu. Young Brody mimicks dad's anxious gestures, in one of those light, humorous dinner scenes that Spielberg does so well. Macho man Quint crushes his beer can in his hand, and Hooper copies him weakly by crushing his paper cup.

The contrast between the three main characters is particularly well handled

Left: Spielberg in contemplative mood during the filming of *Jaws*. He had begun the film knowing of the commercial failure of *The Sugarland Express*.

Right: The shark comes to the surface and opens wide for the next victim.

Below: Hooper is attacked in his underwater cage by the shark.

Jaws is fundamentally a director's movie, and there is no doubt that Spielberg's direction constituted the most efficient manipulation of mass emotion in the cinema since *Psycho*.

Several sequences have become suspense classics. The terrifying opening sequence, in which a girl swimmer (Susan Backlinie) is attacked and killed by the shark, exemplifies several aspects of the film's style: the use of music to anticipate imminent danger; the use of the camera to suggest the threat of the shark without showing it; and the deceptive structure of a number of scenes, in which an initially humorous tone is then displaced by an atmosphere heavy with menace and then finally dissipated entirely by a shark attack. An early scene on the beach has a similar development. The police chief's nervousness and refusal to go near the water is first seen in comic

Above: Quint, in a precarious position, prepares to take on the shark single-handed in *Jaws*. His obsession with the shark eventually takes him over the edge.

Left: The three men have successfully baited the shark and now try tiring it out in a desperate chase.

In the scene of Quint's Indianapolis monologue. Before the monologue, Quint and Hooper have been indulging in a kind of verbal arm-wrestling by comparing scars. Brody can only look timidly at his appendix scar, and cannot compete with the kind of image of manhood for which Quint and Hooper are competing. 'Let's drink to our legs,' says Quint drunkenly: in his final struggle with the shark, it will be his legs that will disappear first. When he begins his monologue, he directs it chiefly at the unscarred Brody, the ancient mariner confronting the effete urbanized man with a knowledge of subterranean darkness and horror that nudges the film away from realism toward myth. The Indianapolis speech is an interlude in the film, but an important one. It explains certain aspects of Quint's character, particularly his obsession with the shark which, like Captain Ahab's search for Moby Dick, he is pursuing in a spirit of personal vendetta. There is a peculiar kinship between Quint and the shark. They are both greedy ('pay me, or suffer all winter,' says Quint to the islanders). Like the shark, Quint has a missing tooth which he shows Hooper, who has

Below: Quint (Robert Shaw, left) and Hooper (Richard Dreyfuss, right) pull on the ropes: Brody (Roy Scheider, center) watches, intently. Brody, the urbanized man, eventually kills the shark.

"Let's drink to our legs"
Creates suspense by implying they are going to get eaten

Above: Co-producer Richard Zanuck is surrounded by the merchandise which the success of *Jaws* has generated.

Left: The man of the city against the beast of the deep. Brody and the shark in *Jaws*.

KEEP LINKING. HOW ALL THESE DIRECTIONS CREATE THE FEELING OF UNCERTAINTY + SUSPENSE

KEY = SUSPENSE AT ITS LARGEST IN FILM

earlier found a shark's tooth in the underwater wreck.

After the horror of the monologue, Hooper breaks the spell by singing 'Show me the way to go home.' A common refrain in the film, it is ironic at this moment because they are floating out on the open sea away from the community, but it also anticipates the ending when Brody and Hooper do begin to drift back home. For the first time in the scene, Brody moves to sit down with the two men and join in the song. And it is at this point that Spielberg cuts to a shot outside the boat of the barrels approaching and of the shark preparing to attack – an implication not only of shark as unseen presence but as malign intelligence, calculatedly choosing the right moment to break up the party, smashing the hollow camaraderie of the men and invading their temporary security and home. The stage is set for the final pulsating confrontation, and this little interlude is revealed as both prophetic and ironic: prophetic in the sense that Quint's monologue seems almost a nightmare premonition of his own death; ironic in the sense that, for all the macho boasting of Quint and Hooper, it is Brody, the urbanized cop from New York, who eventually manages to kill the shark.

Spielberg has intimated on a number of occasions that he has never felt *Jaws* to be a particularly personal work. Nevertheless, one can draw a number of parallels with his preceding work: isolating modern man from civilization and forcing him to participate in an elemental struggle, as in *Duel*; establishing a New Yorker hero, out of his milieu, as in *Something Evil*; and interrogating different varieties of manhood, from machismo to emasculation, as in *Duel* and *Sugarland Express*. Although the first part of *Jaws* alludes to a Watergate-type cover-up, the second part chooses to ignore the problem of the community's greed entirely and concentrates on the excitement of the chase. *Jaws* is a film dedicated to restoring communal confidence. It prefers not to analyze the problem, but to annihilate it. Perhaps this partially explains its enormous success: it clearly reflected a national mood. While it is unlikely that Spielberg had this kind of political statement consciously in mind, the tone is very typical. His films invariably have a strictly linear structure, with no flashbacks, and indeed with little sense of the past, and this seems to reflect a young man striding confidently toward the future. Long after the shocks (and sharks) have palled, one can watch *Jaws* for the sheer craft with which it has been put together, and feel pleasure in the way it displaces the clouds of paranoia with a positive optimism. His next film was to do the same – not just triumphantly, but transcendantly.

CLOSE ENCOUNTERS OF THE THIRD KIND

Spielberg said that his love of science fiction 'sprang from being curious about the stars and space travel and wanting to get off the planet – and having a semi-unhappy childhood looking for escape.' The enormous success of *Jaws* put him in a position where he was a bankable proposition to make a film of his choice, and the $20 million Columbia put into *Close Encounters of the Third Kind* contrasts intriguingly with the $500 that Spielberg had spent on his home science-fiction movie about 15 years before.

A first draft of the script had been completed by Paul Schrader, who had taken the situation of a visitation of earth by aliens as a starting-point for an examination of the anguish and psychology of an alienated American Air Force officer. This treatment bequeathed Spielberg his title, but little else, since it was quite opposed to what Spielberg himself intended. He decided to write the screenplay himself ('I can't do any

We are not alone

CLOSE ENCOUNTERS
OF THE THIRD KIND

Above: The evocative poster for *Close Encounters*.

Left: Spielberg with three of the supporting actors in *Close Encounters of the Third Kind*, Bob Balaban, Lance Henriksen and François Truffaut (right).

Above right: The coming of the extraterrestrials is foretold in an Indian religious meeting.

Below right: Gillian (Melinda Dillon) and her son Barry (Cary Guffey), watch Neary (Richard Dreyfuss) construct the shape which is haunting him.

worse,' was his uncharitable comment). In fact, what he wrote was more of a storyboard than a script, especially the last 40 minutes which, as he said, 'is all phantasmagoria, in which the movie practically becomes another movie.'

Richard Dreyfuss was cast again as Spielberg's alter ego. He played Roy Neary, a suburban Everyman. A repair engineer in Indiana, his life is changed by a close encounter of the third kind with extraterrestrials – that is to say, not simply a sighting or evidence of

physical existence but actual contact with the aliens. Teri Garr was cast as Neary's bewildered wife, and Spielberg immediately instructed her to read Bill Owen's book *Suburbia* and choose her wardrobe accordingly. The actress was later to express great admiration for Spielberg's attention to detail, from the numerous hobbies that Neary has lying around his house (suggestive of a magpie, excitable, and with an impressionable mind) to the precise meal the family is having around the table when Neary starts to sculpt his mashed potato into the shape of the mountain that is obsessing him. 'I guess you've noticed something a little strange with Dad,' he says, in a tone of shame-faced abstraction. 'It's okay, though, I'm still Dad.'

The most audacious piece of casting is that of French director François Truffaut in the role of the scientist Lacombe, who is heading the team preparing to make contact with the alien spacecraft. 'I wanted a man-child,' explained Spielberg, 'ingenuous and wise, a father-figure with this very wide-eyed young outlook on life. I didn't want the stoic with the white hair and pipe.' Spielberg was unquestionably influenced in his choice by Truffaut's performances in his own films, *L'Enfant Sauvage/Wild Child* (1970) and *Day for Night* (1973), and the chemistry worked very well. Interestingly, Spielberg's films share many of the characteristics that one cherishes in Truffaut's: a patent love of the cinema, a deep sympathy with children, a basic kind-

Left: The air-traffic controllers can hardly comprehend what they are seeing: UFOs on screen.

Below: Neary is an archetypal Spielberg hero, the ordinary man swept into extraordinary adventure.

Above: *Watch the Skies* was the original title proposed for *Close Encounters*.

Left: The movie's most spectacular special effect – the Mother Ship, the city of lights, prepares to land.

ness and generosity of spirit and a near-complete absence of human evil. When Truffaut saw the film he is said to have loved it and been especially impressed by the fact that there were no bad guys in it.

For its major set-piece of the landing of the Mother Ship, *Close Encounters* utilized a huge abandoned aircraft hangar at Mobile, Alabama. It was shot in conditions of strict secrecy that ironically parallels those of government and science departments concerning the existence or otherwise of UFOs, a secrecy that the film is at pains to criticize. The UFOs were created by Carlo Rambaldi and played by 50 six-year-old girls. 'E.T.'s,' Spielberg could be heard shouting, when he was directing the scene of the landing of the space ship, 'stop fooling around!' In order to achieve the sympathetic yet unearthly effect he wanted from their appearance, Spielberg photographed them against a furnace of light which 'distorted the humanoid images and made them even more pipe-cleanerish in appearance.' The Mother Ship itself was created by Douglas Trumbull and was conceived by Spielberg as a 'city of lights.' 'Let there be light' was a constant demand. *Close Encounters* finally required more electricians than any film for a decade, lighting an area four times bigger than the largest soundstage.

The coming of the alien is a situation that is familiar from the science fiction movies of the 1950s, where Martian invariably meant Marxist, but *Close Encounters* is about the wonder rather than the terror of the unknown. Typically, Spielberg chooses to express this through the baffled feelings of an ordinary man whose life suddenly turns into an extraordinary adventure. There is grandeur and enigma in the telling; he finds himself with a mysterious facial burn and haunted by the shape of a mountain, which turns out to be Devil's Tower in Wyoming where the American army is preparing for a UFO landing. But there is also humor and eccentricity, unusual in such an epic project. When the aliens first arrive, a child's toys become manically animated. A grudging American voice can be heard opining that 'they can fly rings around the moon, but we're years ahead of them on the highway.' In the best effect, when the lights of a UFO appear behind Neary's car and he casually waves it on as if it were an errant motorist, the lights rise *over* his car, rather than passing him. (When reading the script, Dreyfuss said that this was his favorite scene: he could *hear* the audience reacting.) Neary's gathering absorption with the extraterrestrials climaxes in a mad sequence when he collects gravel and garbage from the garden in order to build a model of the mountain in his living room. It is around this point that wife and children decide that enough is enough and move out. Neary will resume the search with Gillian (Melinda Dillon) who has also had a close encounter and whose son (Cary Guffey) has been spirited away by the aliens.

Close Encounters is a celebration of cinema. This is most immediately felt in the reference to other movies. *The Ten Commandments* (1956) is showing on television (because of its length, Neary is planning only to let his children see five), and Spielberg's film not only matches it for technique – the landing of

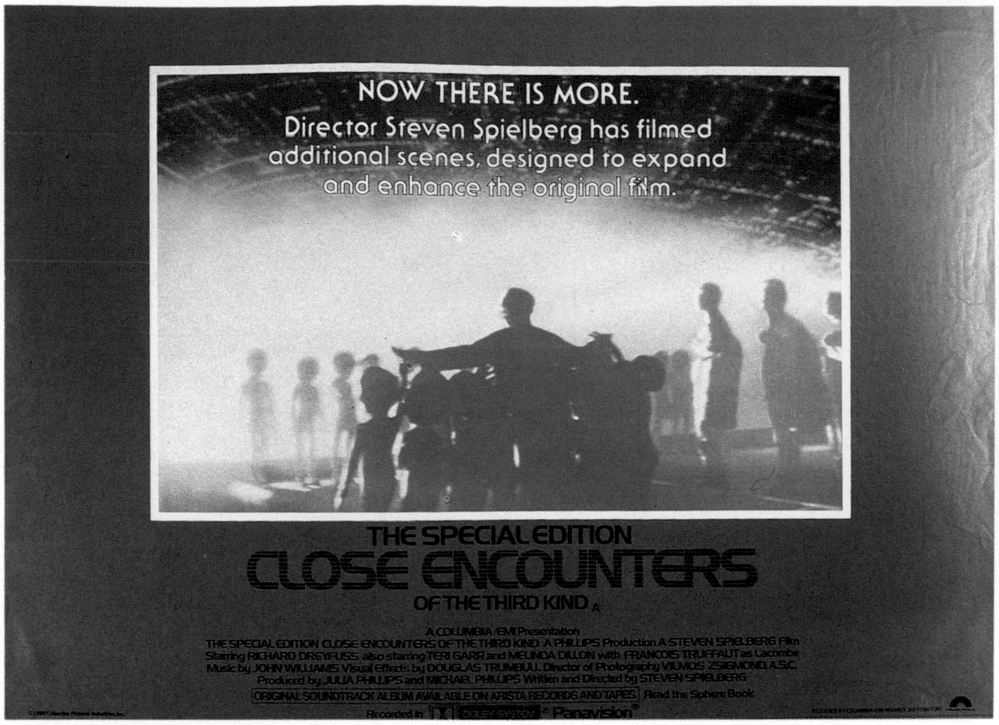
NOW THERE IS MORE.
Director Steven Spielberg has filmed additional scenes, designed to expand and enhance the original film.
THE SPECIAL EDITION
CLOSE ENCOUNTERS
OF THE THIRD KIND
A COLUMBIA/EMI Presentation
THE SPECIAL EDITION CLOSE ENCOUNTERS OF THE THIRD KIND A PHILLIPS Production A STEVEN SPIELBERG Film
Starring RICHARD DREYFUSS also starring TERI GARR and MELINDA DILLON with FRANCOIS TRUFFAUT as Lacombe
Music by JOHN WILLIAMS Visual Effects by DOUGLAS TRUMBULL Director of Photography VILMOS ZSIGMOND A.S.C.
Produced by JULIA PHILLIPS and MICHAEL PHILLIPS Written and Directed by STEVEN SPIELBERG
ORIGINAL SOUNDTRACK ALBUM AVAILABLE ON ARISTA RECORDS AND TAPES
Read the Sphere Book
Recorded in DOLBY SYSTEM
Panavision

Above: The poster for the special edition of *Close Encounters of the Third Kind* contains footage of the interior of the giant spaceship which Spielberg had deleted from the original film.

the Mother Ship being the cinema's most spectacular special effect since de Mille's parting of the Red Sea – it surpasses it in its religious sense of awe. Hitchcock is also evoked, particularly *North by Northwest* (1959), when Neary and Gillian are chased across a mountainside by a low-flying helicopter. More than its allusions to other films, however, *Close Encounters* celebrates cinema in the way it incorporates the film experience into the action proper. The movie begins in darkness, until a blinding flash of light initiates the magical experience. It plays on the proximity of science and cinema, both of which represent triumphs of technology. It is a film whose primary aim is to pack the frame with emotionally dazzling and overwhelming imagery, and to communicate in the way communication is established with the extraterrestrials – not through words but through a harmonious combination of music and signs. Its effect is perhaps most intensely cinematic in the sense of being communal, a shared mass experience, annihilating the private and paltry televisual experience which is often quizzically observed in Spielberg's films as influencing behavior and thought, and deadening the mind.

Close Encounters could not work, would be meaningless, without a mass audience, and Spielberg's power on screen might be dangerous if his message were different. His message is basically one of love, not hate: indeed the grandeur of *Close Encounters* is achieved with a remarkable shortage of conflict. The message is also one of escape. Neary's home background is as crucial thematically as the final spectacular effects: his look to the skies is his way of escaping the blandness of suburbia. Cinema also provides an escape, is also a means of realizing one's dreams, transporting one to another world. *Close Encounters* is Spielberg's ultimate dream-machine, yet also is a curiously intimate epic. It takes us back to his opening comment about 'wanting to get off the planet and having a semi-unhappy childhood to escape.' Cinema gives him the means of creating his own planet, his own world, and *Close Encounters* comes up with a formulation of new families (reunion of mother and child, Neary adopted by the extraterrestrials) that might restore a lost happiness. 'The movie is very gentle,' said Spielberg, contrasting it with the paranoia of 1950s science fiction, 'I wanted it to feel like an embrace.'

The huge success of the movie enabled Spielberg three years later to supervise a special edition of *Close Encounters* for release. The main difference was the tightening of the midsection, including the cutting of Neary's digging up the garden, and the decision to show the inside of the Mother Ship,

Right: Neary is adopted by the extraterrestrials in *Close Encounters*.

Previous pages: The scientists watch in awe the spectacular light show prior to the landing of the Mother Ship.

Above: Gillian (Melinda Dillon) watches the arrival of the UFOs.

Below: Spielberg rehearses the interrogation scene between Richard Dreyfuss (left), François Truffaut and Bob Balaban.

now accompanied over the soundtrack by 'When You Wish upon a Star' from *Pinocchio* (originally in the film but cut after the disappointing first preview). Basically the grand design remains the same: it is less a revision than a re-

release. It was to provide the seed for *E.T.* and seemed to demonstrate that, with two mega-hits in a row, Spielberg's horizons were limitless. However, with his next film, Spielberg was to be the man who fell to earth.

George Lucas made a succinct and perceptive comment on *1941*: 'Steve's direction was brilliant. The idea was terrible.' That is about the size of it, and thereby hangs quite a tale. The script of *1941* was the work of Bob Gale and Robert Zemeckis, whose debut film a year earlier, *I Wanna Hold Your Hand* (1978) had also been Spielberg's debut as an executive producer. *1941* was originally to have

Left: Toshiro Mifune as Commander Mitamura in *1941*. Spielberg was very keen to work with Mifune, famous for his appearances in the Samurai films of Akira Kurosawa.

Below: A promotional still for *1941*; John Belushi admirably conveys its mad, mad, mad, mad atmosphere.

been directed by John Milius, whose writing on a film like John Huston's *The Life and Times of Judge Roy Bean* (1972) and direction of *The Wind and the Lion* (1975) suggested a sensibility well attuned to the script's predilection for wild satire and violent action. However, when Milius began directing *Big Wednesday* (1978), he assumed the role of executive producer on *1941* instead and Spielberg became the director. Spielberg's earlier films had shown a gift for comedy, but of an understated gentle kind rather than the *National Lampoon* style required here. One of the problems is that he never seems to find that bedrock of realism from which he can gradually escalate into farce. *1941* starts loud and frantic, and just becomes louder and more frantic.

The script was inspired by three actual historical events; the sighting of a Japanese submarine off the coast of Santa Barbara in 1942; the consequent 'Great Los Angeles Air Raid,' in which, as a result of the panic provoked by the submarine sighting, the gun-toting inhabitants of LA peppered the sky with bullets for hours without any evidence that there was anything up there; and the fights that broke out in 1943 between sailors and the so-called zoot-suiters, civilians who had not enlisted. The script steamrollers these events into a single interconnecting happening on a single night, which might be overloading the situation to begin with. Apparently, what immediately attracted Spielberg was the Japanese story, and the opportunity

Previous pages: The spectacular aerial fight along the illuminated streets of Hollywood Boulevard, intended by Spielberg as a kind of joke reference to the battles in the air in *Star Wars*.

Right: Civilians and women are about to be caught up in military and male paranoia.

this would afford for working with the great Toshiro Mifune. He was also drawn to the theme of paranoia. Having vanquished paranoia in *Duel, Jaws* and *Close Encounters, 1941* seemed to offer the chance of sending it up and even celebrating it.

1941 is Spielberg's *Apocalypse Now*, an epic egoistic extravagance on a war theme. Its budget of $26.5 million works out at roughly a million dollars a laugh – and that is a generous estimate. It is also Spielberg's *War of the Worlds*, his equivalent to Orson Welles's famous radio production in 1938 about Martians invading America which sent half the country into wild panic. There is an undeniable zip about some of the film's choreographic comedy, its stylistic pastiche, its period charm. Its parody of military clichés and tough-guy dialogue ('Eat lead, slant,' says John Belushi's mad pilot as he engages in an aerial dogfight along the Hollywood Boulevard with what he mistakenly thinks is the enemy) is often funny. So too is the stage-by-stage process by which the

Ned Beatty character, in his determination to defend his home, completely dismantles the whole structure, so that a final nail in the door will send the whole house sliding down a hill. The big comic set-piece is a jitterbug contest which develops into a huge Fordian knockabout between soldiers and sailors. It is done with enormous rhythm and verve, and its depiction of the lunacy whereby Americans expend

their energies in fighting each other rather than the enemy is absolutely germane to the theme. But it is noticeable that, while one is admiring the

Below: The Douglases (Ned Beatty, center, and Lorraine Gray, right) are visited by Sergeant Tree (Dan Aykroyd).

Right: Belushi as 'Wild Bill' Kelso, a daredevil pilot dementedly searching for enemy aircraft.

Previous page: The military prepare to rouse the populace into supporting an attack on the submarine.

skill with which Spielberg guides his camera and his effects, one is not laughing. Why?

Part of the reason is that one is not permitted to care about any of the people involved. In his previous films, as we have seen, Spielberg has followed an absolutely clear single narrative thread: even the more complicated lines of *Close Encounters* ultimately converge on the same spot. But *1941* has a fractured narrative structure, with innumerable isolated set-pieces that remain separate in effect rather than cumulative and the audience is not given any single plot development with which to identify. Spielberg also feels that he allowed the actors too much freedom. There are some nice cameos: Slim Pickens's Christmas tree vendor swallows a compass rather than allowing it to fall into the hands of the enemy; Warren Oates's mad Colonel suspects every tall soldier as being a Japanese on stilts; or Robert Stack's lachrymose Major, mopping away his tears at a cinema showing of *Dumbo* while all hell is breaking loose outside. But too much of the film seems to be a competitive shouting-match among the cast, and Spielberg confessed in retrospect that

'all the actors seemed to get caught up in that kind of civic madness. No one wanted to be normal, as much as I tried to normalize certain relationships.'

Uncharacteristically, Spielberg probably miscalculated the mood of his audience. In the early 1970s, the exuberant anarchy of the film might have appealed to the nation's anti-authoritarian mood generated by dismay over Vietnam and disgust over Watergate. By 1979 America seemed less sympathetic to such criticism and seemed desirous of a rest from self-examination and of a restoration of national pride and heroes. The mood had moved a long way from *M*A*S*H* (1970) and by the end of the decade, military lunacy seemed more a source of sorrow than satire.

One might argue that Los Angeles's over-reaction to a non-existent crisis in *1941* is paralleled by the film's own crazy disproportion between means and ends, that, in a sense, the style mirrors the content. Yet Spielberg has not the wickedness for satire and, as well as

Right: Treat Williams plays the belligerent soldier Sitarski; here he takes part in a jitterbug contest.

Below: John Candy as Foley, with his little furry friend. Spielberg exploits the humor of toys and inanimate objects in *1941*.

Left: Dan Aykroyd (left) and John Belushi (right) in *1941*. Note the prominence of the poster for *Dumbo*, the film Stilwell watches at the cinema while all hell is breaking loose outside.

Right: Captain Birkhead (Tim Matheson) tries to tempt General Stilwell's secretary (Nancy Allen) into a plane.

being a self-indulgent film, *1941* also comes over as a curious exercise in self-parody. It begins with a take-off of the opening of *Jaws* in which a nude female bather (again played by Susan Backlinie) is now menaced by a mechanical Leviathan in the form of a Japanese submarine. Although it evokes classic Hollywood in its re-creation of period, notably the slapstick satires of Preston Sturges, *1941* is actually an archetype of the megalomania of modern Hollywood. Millions are spent on indulging the esoteric extravagance of the superstar director and more millions are spent on creating artifacts whose sole purpose is to be blown up in an orgy of destruction. When the Japanese mistake the amusement park on Santa Monica for the whole of Hollywood ('Fire at that industrial structure!' roars Mifune's commander), a comment is surely being made on the epic frivolousness of modern Hollywood. It is a fair comment, but it is an odd comment from Steven Spielberg, of all people, to be making, and even odder in the context of the wasteful excesses of *1941*.

'The film does cater to the lowest moral character in all of us,' said Spielberg, 'without licking the sewer. It's just a tongue's reach away from good sewer humor, but falls short of classic comedy.' What united the characters, he said, was the intensity of their wants – whether it was a girl, security, peace or war – and their pursuit of this desire results in a comic pile-up of exploded dreams. It is a promising concept, but somehow juvenile innuendo, crude misogyny and predictable pacing have all contrived to jam the mechanism. There is a hint of *Catch 22* in its thesis on the insanity of conflict, but the theme seems to be lost in the babble and blur of pointless action.

1941 is a talented failure, but a failure nonetheless. It is perhaps a mark of this failure that, in the midst of all the spectacle – aerial combat, sliding houses – the best jokes are almost incidental: a ventriloquist's dummy spotting the Japanese menace before his operator; and the difficulty the Japanese have in fitting Slim Pickens's confiscated radio into their submarine hatch. Looking at the cumbersome machine, the Japanese sailor comments thoughtfully 'We've got to figure out a way to make these things smaller.'

Below: A Christmas tree salesman, Hollis Wood (Slim Pickens, center) has fallen into the hands of the Japanese. Here he is being threatened by Commander Matamura (Toshiro Mifune, left). At one point Wood swallows a compass rather than let it fall into the hands of the Japanese.

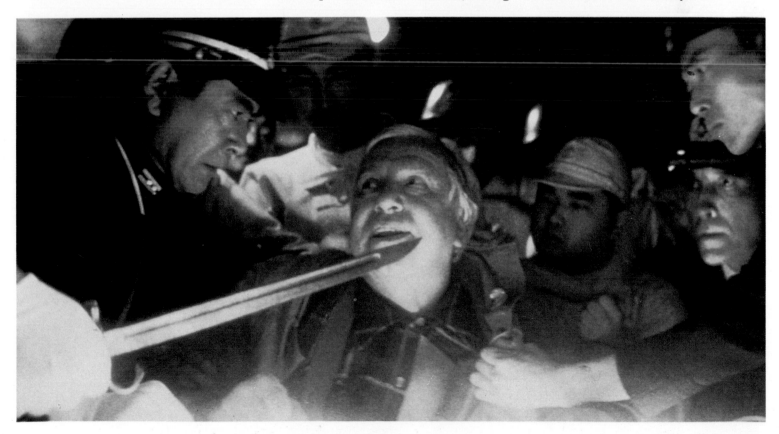

RAIDERS OF THE LOST ARK

Although they had been friends for years, George Lucas and Steven Spielberg had never collaborated on a film before. However, during a now-famous Hawaiian vacation they spent together in May 1977, when Lucas was apprehensively awaiting the opening of his new film, *Star Wars*, and Spielberg was taking a break from the rigors of *Close Encounters*, they came up with an idea that later became *Raiders of the Lost Ark*. Lucas had the conception of the Indiana Jones hero, and Spielberg the desire to make a film that corresponded to the adventure serials he had enjoyed at the cinema as a child. With writer-director Philip Kaufman (who was later to make a superb film of Tom Wolfe's *The Right Stuff*), Lucas had

fashioned a story that combined the legend of the lost Ark of the Covenant with Hitler's known fascination with occult and religious artifacts. Spielberg recommended Lawrence Kasdan to write the screenplay on the basis of the script Kasdan had submitted for a forthcoming Spielberg production, *Continental Divide* (1981).

'If a person can tell me the idea in 25 words or less,' Spielberg said, 'it's going to make a pretty good movie. I like ideas, especially movie ideas, that you can hold in your hand.' Critic David Castell's crisp summary of the idea of *Raiders of the Lost Ark* is about 10 words too long by Spielberg's criterion, but admirably summarizes the whole movie: 'Indiana Jones is an archaeologist involved in a race to prevent the

Ark of the Covenant from falling into the hands of the Nazis, who will then become invincible and win World War Two.' The potential politics of the story did not interest Spielberg in the slightest, for him, it was just goodies and baddies. *Raiders of the Lost Ark* was simply designed to be the most explosive and rip-roaring adventure movie seen in the cinema for an extremely long time.

Below: Spielberg plays with his multi-million dollar toy, movies. *Raiders* made elaborate use of miniatures and special effects.

Opposite: The face of the 1980's screen hero – Harrison Ford as Indiana Jones.

Above: Indiana Jones and Marion (Karen Allen) find themselves sealed in a well alive with snakes.

Left: Lawrence Kasdan scripted *Raiders of the Lost Ark*. He is one of a number of talented film people whose path into the industry has been eased by Spielberg's encouragement.

Far left: Indiana Jones lowers himself into the crypt which contains the coveted Lost Ark.

Below: Indy has to outrun a giant boulder.

The opening sequence (to describe it as 'action-packed' would be an absurd understatement) was Lucas's idea. The famous logo of the Paramount mountain fades into an actual mountain on a South American location, and a group of intrepid adventurers shuffle into the frame with their backs to us. It is some time before we have a good look at the hero (we see his whip before we see his face). However, within the first 15

minutes, he will survive an attempt on his life; be clambered over by a tarantula; vault a terrifying ravine; be chased by a giant boulder; fall into the clutches of an arch enemy Belloq (Paul Freeman), and be compelled to surrender the valuable idol for which he has risked his life; be chased through undergrowth by marauding natives; and be rescued by a waiting plane only to find himself being embraced by the pet snake of the pilot.

The point about this opening is that it has very little to do with the plot that follows but everything to do with the style one can expect. It introduces us to the resourcefulness and athleticism of the hero, while also establishing some of his vulnerable traits (his hatred of snakes, his readiness to trust people who will betray him). It also introduces his enemy, Belloq, who is similarly obsessed with the Ark and entranced by Jones's girlfriend Marion (Karen Allen)

Left: Indy continues the chase for the Lost Ark on horseback. At times the film leaps from chase to chase with no real logic.

Right: With great care, Indiana Jones lifts a priceless Indian relic. He will later be cheated of it by his dedicated rival, Belloq.

Below: Indy prepares to deal in peremptory fashion with a show-off wielding a scimitar.

Left: Indy and Marion are tied up while Belloq and the Nazis prepare to perform a ceremony which will open the Ark and unleash its powers for their benefit.

Right: Where Indy goes, explosions are sure to follow. Breaking out from capture, he and Marion once again create havoc among their enemies.

Below: Belloq (Paul Freeman) stares in horror as he realizes the destructive force of the power he has released.

adults who have grown up with a more suggestive, restrained approach to violence in the cinema.

Although less secure than *Jaws* in its integration of adventure, humor and suspense, *Raiders* can be enjoyed as a rousing collage of skeletons, snakes and special effects. It has a *Citizen Kane*-like ending, in which the Ark is seen being stored amid an infinity of packing cases (for future use by the American Government?). The idea was Philip Kaufman's, and it does not really match the hell-for-leather tone, but closing the film on a diminuendo of intrigue is satisfyingly unexpected. Harrison Ford's leading performance combines the grumpy, sometimes grubby, charm of a Bogart with the acrobatic panache of a Burt Lancaster. It is surprising to recall that he only landed the role when the original choice, Tom Selleck, was unable to obtain clearance from his *Magnum* contract. Douglas Slocombe's photograph is richly shaded, and John Williams drives the action along with his punchy and appropriate musical score.

In short, *Raiders* can best be appreciated as a celebration of two things that are closely akin: American energy, and popular movies that provide an adventure and escape that one rarely encounters in real life. Of course, the art of providing that is very hard work. The most delightful, offhand joke in *Raiders* is undoubtedly the moment where Jones deals with a demonic dervish, who is arrogantly whirling his fiendish scimitar in anticipation of a vivid struggle. Originally in the script, this was to be a mammoth confrontation but, by the time the scene arrived, both Ford and Spielberg were so exhausted by the location that they opted for a simpler solution, 'Let's just shoot him,' they agreed – and they did.

Left: E.T. and Elliott emerge from luxuriant undergrowth in a publicity shot for E.T.

Above: The children accompany and protect E.T. The film made expressive use of shadow, and created a charged, magical atmosphere. The cameraman Allen Daviau had worked with Spielberg on *Amblin'*.

Right: The famous bicycle chase in *E.T.*

The above description might suggest a charming fairy-tale but it does not account for the film's extraordinary success. How does Spielberg succeed in involving an audience so totally in his fantasy? This is a complex question, and there are many facets to the answer. Certainly John Williams's music has a vital role to play. Williams had composed the music for every one of Spielberg's feature films. In *Jaws*, the music was the film's own anxious heartbeat; in *E.T.* it is its emotional soul, lifting the spirits of both characters and audience with themes of soaring Americana. Then there are Spielberg's particular gifts as a director: his wonderful story sense, his instinct for camera placement and his extraordinary facility with both suspense and humor. *E.T.* has one of the most immediately compelling narrative structures – a combination of discovery and escape, of chase and rescue. It is literally uplifted by some delightful imagery, notably the cycle chase which

suddenly takes to the skies so that the shadow of a bike can be seen soaring across the moon.

Unlike *Close Encounters*, *E.T.* does not dazzle you with its special effects: indeed, in this regard, it is a rather subdued and intimate film. What dazzles you is the intensity with which Spielberg forces you to identify with the children's world. Spielberg has claimed that *E.T.* is 'about the views and values of modern American kids' which, on the face of it, seems rather strange and more appropriate to the original *After School* idea than the final *E.T.* Yet Spielberg probably means that, for the child, a friendly fantasy world might be more vivid, more real than the real world itself, and that it is in this fantasy world that the child's values and ideals are particularly enacted. In both *Close Encounters* and *Poltergeist*, it is children who make the first contact with the alien, irrational world because they still trust their instincts whereas the adults have lost that sixth sense.

In *E.T.* Spielberg attempts to rediscover the child in every adult. He does this not simply by underplaying the adults' roles in the film but by shooting most of the action at a child's eye level. The participants in the sinister search for E.T. are all photographed from the waist or knees down – the leader of the search (Peter Coyote) is identified not by his face but by the keys he is carrying – and it is a long time in the film before a man is seen in full shot. Spielberg likened this technique to that of cartoons, where the presence of adults is frequently indicated by an arm or legs rather than their whole body. The effect is to compel an audience to see the action through children's eyes. In so doing, and with a narrative that plays on so many primal themes and emotions, the audience is invited to embark on a journey back into their own childhood.

Underlying *E.T.* are a lot of potent myths, very skilfully blended together: Peter Pan, Babes in the Wood, the fantasy of friendly otherworldly creatures who can work miracles but who also need human protection from human aggression. Much of the emotional power of *E.T.* comes from the situation of the broken family of both E.T. and Elliott, and the search for some way of repairing this break or finding alternative emotional fulfilment in an ideal friendship. There is also the hint of a religious subtheme in the resurrection of E.T., his discovery by Elliott in a kind of stable and the name of Elliott's mother being Mary. Even the sub-

Left: A bicycle soars across the moon as E.T. uses a little levitation to escape with Elliott from their pursuers.

Above: Gertie (Drew Barrymore) and Mary (Dee Wallace) in *E.T.* Mary is a typical mother character in Spielberg, compelled to bring up her children alone.

Below: The spacecraft has returned, and Elliott and E.T. prepare for one of the most emotional farewell scenes in movies. However, Spielberg avoided falling into sentimentality.

Right: The spacecraft takes off. So did the film, rapidly becoming one of the biggest box-office hits of all time. It was Spielberg's most personal film to date, the closest to his own sensibilities.

Michelangelo graphics for the film's poster have a religious dimension.

E.T. could have slipped either into a pond of pretentiousness or a slough of sentimentality, and Spielberg is the only director with the emotional innocence and stylistic sophistication necessary to make the material work. It is clear that the subject of child-like wish-fulfilment appealed to him, as did the humor he could extract from the adults' loss of precisely that kind of child-like wonder and faith (notably in the superb scene when Elliott's mother is so overladen with adult rationalism that she is literally unable to see a drunken alien staggering around her kitchen). It gave him the opportunity for a fresh fantasy so inventive and memorable that it could instantly be assimilated into modern mythology (all the succeeding jokes about E.T. phoning home). The amazing thing is that he attracted such masses to a film that is not only without violence but also without villains. It is, in Spielberg's words, a 'happily pacifistic film,' a song of joy from a peerless popular artist who can sing it as if he believed every note. Only a heart of stone could not find it irresistible.

INDIANA JONES AND THE TEMPLE OF DOOM

1984

After the rampant worldwide success of *Raiders of the Lost Ark*, there was never any doubt that there would have to be another Indiana Jones adventure. After the fun Spielberg had had making *Raiders*, there was never any doubt that he would direct it. Besides, he and Lucas were still determined to display something they had planned for *Raiders* but had not managed to include: namely, the awesome spectacle of archaeologist-adventurer Indiana Jones in an immaculate dinner jacket.

The team Lucas and Spielberg assembled contained many of the original technical personnel of *Raiders*. Lucas once again masterminded the production and wrote the original story; Douglas Slocombe was again in charge of photography; and there were additionally two indispensable members of the Spielberg entourage – composer John Williams and editor Michael Kahn (who had edited every Spielberg movie since *Close Encounters*). However, there were also some fresh faces in the team and some novelties in the

Above: Ke Huy Quan plays Short Round in *Indiana Jones*, a Chinese orphan Indy adopts. Spielberg scoured the world to find the child for this part: he finally discovered him in Los Angeles.

Left: The poster for *Indiana Jones*. The slogan says it all. After a period of self-doubt in the 1970s, American cinema has discovered heroes again and Indiana Jones fits the bill admirably.

Right: Spielberg directs Ke Huy Quan in the underground temple.

material. This time the screenplay was in the hands of Willard Huyck and Gloria Katz, still most celebrated for their splendid script for *American Graffiti*. Indiana Jones was again played by Harrison Ford, who had made the part his own in *Raiders*. (Both the original choice, Tom Selleck and a seasoned campaigner like Burt Lancaster are on record as paying generous praise to Ford's performance). But this time Indy had two new helpmates, a nightclub singer Willie Scott (Kate Capshaw)

Above: Spielberg directs Kate Capshaw in her role as Willie Scott, an American night-club singer.

Left: Indy in the spectacular opening night-club scene, where the chorus sings an Oriental version of 'Anything Goes.'

and a Chinese orphan Indy has adopted, Short Round (Ke Huy Quan), a deceptively frail-looking child who is actually an expert in karate. Spielberg had searched world wide for someone to play Short Round, but he actually found the boy he wanted in Los Angeles. Spielberg was so impressed by Quan's performance in *Indiana Jones* that he later appeared in the Spielberg production, *The Goonies.*

Strictly speaking, *Indiana Jones* is a prequel to *Raiders* not a sequel, since the action opens a year earlier than that of the preceding film, in 1935. Like *Raiders*, the new film begins with a spectacular set-piece that has not much relevance to the main narrative but has the effect of seizing the attention of the audience in an instant iron-grip. The setting is the Obi Wan nightclub in Shanghai, where Indy is awaiting payment for services rendered in the form of a precious diamond. On stage is a brilliant production number of Cole Porter's 'Anything Goes,' shrouded in

Below: Indiana, Willie and Short Round flee from gang boss Lao Che in a rubber dinghy.

Above: Willie (Kate Capshaw) in the thick of the action. Generally the heroine is less spunky than in *Raiders*, more of a conventional romantic than a tomboy.

scarlet smoke, sung in Chinese, and in which the combination of choreographic eccentricity and sultry eroticism suggests a bizarre but breathtaking stylistic marriage between Busby Berkeley and Josef von Sternberg.

Needless to say, it is not long before the film is indeed demonstrating that anything goes. As Indy is cheated out of his diamond (it is lost among the sugar cubes) and almost poisoned, Spielberg contrives a balletic night-club brawl similar to the dance-hall chaos of *1941*. With Willie and Short Round in tow, Indy is then chased around the narrow streets and back alleys of Shanghai. They all escape by cargo plane, which Indy then has to abandon over the Himalayas in order to avoid landing in the territory of his enemy, and transform a rubber dinghy into a parachute to save himself and his two companions. On landing in India, they are greeted as

saviors by local villagers who believe the three have been providentially sent to rediscover the sacred Sankara stone which the villagers think will lift the curse of famine and misery from their homes. The search for the stone will lead Indy and his two friends to the Temple of Doom and into more perilous

adventures involving human sacrifice and slavery before the stone is returned.

Obviously the plot is basically an artful juggling of bits and pieces of essentially Victorian colonial adventures, alternately evoking Wilkie Collins, Rider Haggard and *Gunga Din*. Spielberg deliberately, perhaps con-

Right: Having discovered he has no gun, Indiana has to grapple with the murderous thugees at close quarters.

Left: Suspense on a suspension bridge. Willie and Short Round hang on.

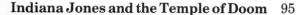

Left: Indiana and Short Round trapped in the dreaded spike chamber.

Previous pages: A gentle scene around the campfire with Indiana and Short Round. An elephant looks on, impassively.

troversially, makes no attempt to update the conventions of such tales to take into account the increased sensitivity nowadays to the racial and sexual stereotyping characteristic of these stories. The portraiture of the Thuggees in *Indiana Jones* is intended to be taken no more seriously than Spielberg's comic-strip Nazis in *Raiders*, though whether that justifies the characterization is perhaps a moot point. Similarly the stereotype of the screaming heroine would certainly not appeal to modern feminists but is very much part of the tradition. Spielberg tries to lighten this by comic incongruity. Willie worries about her nails while snakes and jungle insects crawl around her; she sprinkles perfume on her elephant for a more aromatic ride; and complains about 'foreign food' when they are entertained in the Pleasure Pavilion of the Palace of Pankot with an array of dishes that includes live snake pie, eyeball soup and tandoori beetle. On the whole, though, the character is less spunky than Karen Allen's heroine in *Raiders*, and certainly less enterprising than Kathleen Turner's heroine in *Romancing the Stone* (1984), an *Indiana Jones*-lookalike movie that was being directed at more or less the same time by Spielberg's protegé, Robert Zemeckis.

In some respects, *Indiana Jones* represents a definite advance on *Raiders*. It is more elaborately fantasized, the visual humor is better timed, and Ford's performance has greater ease and wit. In terms of action, the mixture is more or less the same as before, with one spectacular set-piece succeeding the next as if someone's thumb is stuck on a fast-forward button. The perils this time include a sinister spike chamber that can crush its inhabitants to death if the right lever is not found in time, and a fiery furnace into which Willie is being lowered before Indy's timely rescue. The two outstanding set-pieces are a riveting chase in an underground railway after Indy, Willie and Short Round have liberated the child slaves from the Temple and are being pursued by the nasty Thuggees; and an acrobatic crossing of a ricketty rope bridge that spans a gorge with a menacing drop of over 300 feet.

'The Hero is Back' proclaimed the posters for *Indiana Jones*, and it is clear that once again Spielberg had gauged to a nicety the tastes of contemporary

movie audiences, particularly those in America, who were in the mood again for traditional heroics and to whom Indiana Jones seemed an engaging blend of Errol Flynn and James Bond. Indiana Jones is no superman: he relies on bravado and bluff as much as strength and often has to pull himself through by his wits and his will more than by muscular might. This human, vulnerable dimension undoubtedly made him more endearing and believable to audiences. It would be no exaggeration to say that the successful return of the Hero in *Indiana Jones* paved the way for heroes like Rambo and Rocky, in the following year, to ride triumphantly to the rescue of the American Dream.

Yet there was a note of doubt in some critical minds about Spielberg's achievement in *Indiana Jones and the Temple of Doom*. Some of the doubts

were similar to those raised in the discussion about *Raiders*: the questionable violence; the insensitivity of some of the characterization; the disproportion between means (the colossal budget) and ends (a movie with aspirations little more advanced than those of the old Saturday serials). Some of the worries had to do with Spielberg's continuing commitment to the cinema of sensation, and how long it could last. As the veteran director Martin Ritt commented: 'The young kids coming up, they all seem totally into sensation. They don't have a literary tradition and they equate everything with the grosses. But it just can't go on. You can't keep whipping that same old meringue without it finally exploding in your face.' For some Spielberg admirers, *Indiana Jones* was a somewhat disappointing and even disturbing development. The hero might be back, but is it not a much more conventional and less original concept of heroism than that of earlier Spielberg movies like *Duel, Sugarland Express, Jaws* or *Close Encounters* – movies, moreover, that operated and provided pleasure on much more than one simple, visceral level?

Perhaps this is being too harsh, and trying to strangle Spielberg's own perception of his development in much the same way as critics have sometimes

Left: The rope bridge, which is cut, clung to, climbed, but rarely crossed in its remarkable appearance in the film.

Right: The Temple of Doom, in which human sacrifices are made, the thugee cult revived and prayers are offered for the discovery of the Sankara stone which will give the evil goddess Kali absolute power.

Below: Indiana with the powerful sacred Sankara stone in his possession at last.

tried to strangle that of Woody Allen. Why should the director fit into the critics' pigeonholed perception of him? The appeal of *Indiana Jones* plainly lies in its desire to give everyone back his youth, providing adventure for the young and reminding older patrons of the serials they enjoyed in their childhood. The success of the movie would make it ridiculous to talk of Spielberg's decline: it would be better to call it conscious regression. One could not fault his skill at making movies for children of all ages. Just occasionally, however, one could wish that someone with such prodigious talent and intelligence might be more intellectually ambitious. Was it not time for Spielberg to make an adult movie for adults? Encouragingly, the evidence would soon suggest that Spielberg had been asking himself much the same sort of questions, and drawing the same sort of conclusions.

THE SPIELBERG PRODUCTIONS

A consideration of those films in which Spielberg has served as producer or executive producer rather than director is necessary in order to round out one's impression of his contribution to modern Hollywood. To begin with, these productions have allowed Spiel-

Left: Beatlemania in *I Wanna Hold Your Hand*. It was Spielberg's first production and was directed by Robert Zemeckis.

Below: Nancy Allen (center) leads the Beatles' fans who invade New York when the 'Fab Four' visit in 1964.

berg to sponsor new talents and ease and encourage their route into direction. 'I have a general philosophy,' he once said, 'you have to put back what you take out, or the well runs dry.' Also, they have increased one's awareness of the particular characteristics of Spielberg's film world. In some cases, the director has been allowed to refashion that world in order to satirize and attack it and bring out some of the subterranean elements of suburbia, the homicidal as well as the homely, that Spielberg's own films as director suppress.

His career as producer had a notably

rocky start. Significantly, perhaps, it began while Spielberg was preparing his mega-flop *1941* and his fortunes did not improve until after his return to winning ways as a director with *Raiders of the Lost Ark*. His first two ventures as executive producer were both directed by Robert Zemeckis, from screenplays co-written by Zemeckis and Bob Gale. *I Wanna Hold Your Hand* (1978) was a look at Beatlemania in early 1960s America, the main running joke of which was the wearying number of strategies by which the film avoided showing the Beatles. Spielberg probably thought of it as his equivalent of

Left: John Belushi in *Continental Divide*. Though scripted by Kasdan and directed by Michael Apted, the film was not a success.

Right: A stampede of cars is one of the comic highlights of *Used Cars*, a black comedy directed by Robert Zemeckis.

American Graffiti and that it might cash in on the box-office success of *Saturday Night Fever* (1977), but it did not. Similarly disappointing was *Used Cars* (1980), a black comedy about two brothers (Kurt Russell and Jack Warden) who run rival car lots; the film suffered from an uncertainty and inconsistency of mood. No more successful was his third production, *Continental Divide* (1981), directed by Michael Apted, in which John Belushi and Blair Brown, as newspaperman and ornithologist respectively, make an ill-matched romantic couple. Nevertheless, Spielberg did at least discover a scriptwriter from the experience, Lawrence Kasdan, who was not only to write *Raiders of the Lost Ark*, but also with *Body Heat* (1982), *The Big Chill* (1983) and *Silverado* (1985), quickly establish himself as one of the promising American writer-directors of recent

Below: Tobe Hooper (right) directs a scene from *Poltergeist*, Spielberg's first smash hit as a producer.

years. So Spielberg's talent-spotting was functioning, if not his assessment of box-office trends.

His luck turned with *Poltergeist* (1982), partly, one suspects, because Spielberg wrote the story himself and took a very active role in the making of the film. Although Tobe Hooper is credited with the direction, Spielberg was reportedly almost constantly on the set and giving expert advice. The plot is triggered by a young child's becoming aware of strange voices that seem to emanate from behind the television set. In *Poltergeist* two distinct voices seem to come from *behind* the cinema screen also. Horror specialist Hooper, director of the notorious *Texas Chainsaw Massacre* (1973), highlights the gory and Gothic aspects of the plot: decaying

Right: Diane Freeling (Jobeth Williams) slips in the mud of her partially excavated swimming pool and is greeted by a mound of skeletons and skulls in *Poltergeist*.

Far right: The storms of the supernatural are gathering around the suburban household of the Freelings.

flesh, a floating graveyard, and an emphasis on the violation of sacred burial grounds. More characteristic of Spielberg is the stress on the imagination of the children and the resourcefulness of the mother, the quizzical attitude to television, and the essentially humorous portrayal of the medium. In the end, the Spielberg influence predominates because *Poltergeist* is more genial than gruesome. At the same time, it makes an interesting comparison with *E.T.*, with its sharper observation of suburban mores and of strange visitors who, in this case, might not wish you well.

Spielberg's geniality among a surrounding gruesomeness is also felt in the episode 'Kick the Can' that he directed from *The Twilight Zone* (1983), a portmanteau movie he co-produced

Below: Heather O'Rourke plays Carol Anne Freeling, who seems to hear whispering from inside the TV in *Poltergeist*.

with John Landis. An elderly optimist, Mr Bloom (Scatman Crothers) visits the Sunnyvale Rest Home and, for a night, magically contrives that the old people return to their childhood. Spielberg's direction is perfunctory and the tone excessively sentimental, but the subject intriguingly anticipates Ron Howard's hit comedy, *Cocoon* (1985), and the theme, for Spielberg scholars, is quite interesting. It initially indulges a nostalgia for the past but then begins

to question it. The old people are reminded of some of the pains of childhood – exams, the death of one's parents, the incompleteness of one's life before the meeting with one's husband or wife. The trick, as Mr Bloom says, 'is to be your own true age and keep a young mind.' Spielberg's philosophy in a nutshell.

One of the darker episodes of *The Twilight Zone* film concerns a sinister child who has the capacity to turn car-

Above: Crew and passengers after a frightening flight in *The Twilight Zone*, co-produced by Spielberg with John Landis.

Left: Jeremy Licht as the strange child in *The Twilight Zone*, an eccentric combination of animation and horror directed by Joe Dante, who was to make *Gremlins* for Spielberg.

toon figures into raging monsters. It was directed by Joe Dante and now seems a sort of dress-rehearsal for Dante's direction of the next Spielberg production, *Gremlins* (1984), which was so savage that in England no child under the age of 15 was allowed to see it. What Dante does is to launch a marvellously anarchic, full-scale assault on the cuteness and sentimentality of the Spielberg world. His gremlins are not simply monsters which come alive at night: they are basically rebellious children reacting against the tenets of respectability and good taste espoused by their soft, suburban elders. Chris Columbus's screenplay shows a real understanding of the Spielberg world in its characterization of the family with an ineffectual father; and there is one wonderfully incongruous monologue in which a girl explains her non-belief in Santa Claus through describing the death of her father, suffocated when

Right: Gizmo charms his way into a typical American home in *Gremlins*.

Above: The gremlins get drunk in a bar in *Gremlins*, celebrating Christmas in their own inimitable way.

Right: A gremlin risks triple lung cancer during a night on the town.

trying to climb the chimney in a Father Christmas outfit.

Two scenes are classics. The first is the one in which the mother fights off the gremlins with the instruments in her kitchen, not only another example in Spielberg of maternal resourcefulness but a revelation of the American kitchen as a technological torture-chamber. The second is the scene in which the gremlins break into a cinema, start behaving like a particularly rowdy popcorn matinee audience, and then become enchanted by the film they are watching – needless to say, *Snow White and the Seven Dwarfs*. Disney can even work his spell on gremlins. When a mischievous gremlin pops up behind an E.T. doll, it is clear that Dante has Steven Spielberg firmly in his comic sights, and it is to Spielberg's credit that he nevertheless gave Dante his head to mock Spielberg in this cheeky fashion.

1985 saw two Spielberg productions in circulation, one a relatively modest success, the other a smash-hit. The modest success was *The Goonies*,

Above: The bored children of *The Goonies* are suddenly plunged into perilous adventure. Left is Ke Huy Quan.

directed by the versatile Richard Donner, probably chosen here for his work on fantasies like *Superman* (1978) and *Ladyhawke* (1985). The goonies are seven kids – 'an oddball cross-section of America,' says Donner – who are suddenly launched into perilous adventure when they discover an old pirate map and are chased by some very stagy villains. 'Nothing exciting ever happens around here,' one of the children has said. The adventure is nothing less than a wish fulfilment of excitement in reaction against boring suburbia and ineffectual parent figures, particularly dad. The protracted and sentimental ending not only resolves the adventure but allows the children to save their families from having to vacate their homes to make way for real-estate development. The problem with the movie is its rather relentless escapism – a Disneyland ride is fun, but for two hours? – and the evasiveness of its message. The goonies' adventures are

an escape from suburbia but, in saving their families' homes, are the children not attaching themselves to suburbia even more strongly? By so doing, won't they be facing the same problems again in the near future?

The smash-hit was *Back to the Future* (1985), a reunion between Spielberg and director Robert Zemeckis after the

latter had proved to his own satisfaction that he could succeed without Spielberg's patronage with *Romancing the Stone*. *Back to the Future* is a sprightly fantasy about a young man (Michael J Fox) transported back to the 1950s at a time when the local cinema was showing not porn movies but *Cattle Queen of Montana* (1954) starring Barbara

Right: Marty (Michael J Fox, center) who has returned to the 1950s in *Back to the Future*, explains to Doc (Christopher Lloyd), that Marty's amorous visitor (Lea Thompson) is his future mother.

Stanwyck and a B-picture actor called Ronald Reagan. As well as prematurely introducing the community to rock 'n' roll, Michael J Fox finds himself being romantically pursued by his own mother. One recognizes a lot of Spielberg fingerprints here: the affectionate portrait of small-town America; the primacy of fantasy and the jokes about television; the humor toward yet celebration of the family.

In 1986 Spielberg unveiled three new productions. *Young Sherlock Holmes*, directed by Barry Levinson, is an entertaining if strained yoking together of Conan Doyle Victoriana and Indiana Jones-type adventure. *The Money Pit*, directed by Richard Benjamin, is an updating of the old Cary Grant comedy *Mr Blandings Builds His Dream House*, in which the performing skills of Shelley Long and Tom Hanks tend to be buried under a cacophony of comic catastrophe. *An American Tail*, directed by Don Bluth, is a feature-length cartoon about a family of persecuted Russian mice in 1885 who emigrate to an America whose streets are allegedly paved with cheese. The animation is most impressive but the real interest of *An American Tail* is its final confirmation of Spielberg as the new Walt Disney. The main plot situation (the separation of a child from its parents), and the combination of sentiment and horror (like the moment when a huge wave in a storm suddenly assumes the shape of a sea monster) are indelibly influenced by Disney classics like *Pinocchio* and *Dumbo*.

If Spielberg wishes to be Disney, it seems churlish to insist that he should try to be Orson Welles. Yet, for some critics, Spielberg has become more of a 'confectioner' than creative artist and betrayed his early promise. *The Color Purple* was probably an attempt on Spielberg's part to answer that criticism by tackling a controversial subject and establish himself as a serious director. The response was mixed, but it was a bold attempt, and an encouraging indication of a deepening curiosity about character. It might be that the split in style will gradually widen between the movies he produces – as he puts it, movies he would like to see but not direct – and the movies he personally makes.

THE COLOR PURPLE

'It won't make him a fortune ... but it will probably go down as his most important film ever and the one he's going to be remembered by.' So said the distinguished black American filmmaker Gordon Parks (best known for his films, *The Learning Tree* and *Shaft*) about Spielberg's film, *The Color Purple*. Parks was speaking at the time from a privileged position within the production, for he had been drafted into the movie by Spielberg in a kind of freelance role of observer and advisor – an unusual appointment that indicates perhaps both the seriousness and nervousness with which Spielberg was undertaking his most unusual assignment.

It is probably too early to assess the accuracy of Parks's prediction. Although not a blockbuster, *The Color Purple* has been a respectable commercial success. Its impact on Spielberg's overall critical reputation is more difficult to gauge, for the quality of the film has been somewhat shrouded by the controversy it attracted.

At the outset, one should not underestimate the risk Spielberg was taking. Admittedly, Alice Walker's novel already had the prestige of a Pulitzer Prize behind it, but it is also clearly a novel that would present major difficulties for movie adaptation. It is written in the form of letters, has a time span of 30 years, and has relatively little narrative incident. Alice Walker's wise advice about casting – 'the final cast must seem like they have stepped straight from the book,' she insisted – meant that the movie could not rely on stars for commercial insurance. (In other words, Diana Ross would not have been suitable casting in the role of Shug Avery.)

For Spielberg, it was his first overtly serious film for a decade and a project dependent on the quality of his human insight rather than the majesty of his special effects. Also it was a subject completely outside his own experience: an account of a Negro community in the American South from 1908 to the late 1930s, seen from the viewpoint of an oppressed heroine, Celie, who is the novel's main narrator. The question arises: what was it in the subject that would attract Spielberg in the first place? There is actually more than one might think.

The treatment of family life in *The Color Purple* – the bonds of affection, the bones of contention – would no doubt appeal to Spielberg since, as we have seen, the situation of the fragile or broken family has regularly recurred in his films. Celie's cruel husband in *The Color Purple* – she refers to him imper-

Below: Poster for *The Color Purple*, with Celie enclosed in a consoling purple haze, reading the letters from her beloved sister.

The Color Purple

sonally as 'Mister' and does not discover until much later that his first name is Albert – seems an extension of the insensitive or ineffectual male figures that have been so prominent in Spielberg's work, in films as varied as *Something Evil*, *Duel*, *E.T.*, *Gremlins* and *The Goonies*. Early on in the novel, Celie writes: 'I don't even look at mens. That's the truth. I look at women, tho, cause I'm not scared of them.' The deepest sensitivity in Spielberg's films invariably comes from either women or children, so it is not surprising that he would be drawn to the loving relationship of the sisters Celie and Nettie, and pained by their separation when Albert drives Nettie out of their house and for years hides her letters to Celie. As an inventive story-teller himself, Spielberg would also no doubt have been entranced by the extraordinary twist in the tale, whereby Nettie is taken in by the married couple that has adopted Celie's own two children, sired by and then disposed of by the man Celie has presumed is her father. 'It is a miracle, isn't it?' says Nettie in the novel, 'And no doubt impossible for you to believe.'

Some readers have found this impossible to believe, but one suspects that this dimension of the 'miraculous' would endear the tale all the more to the maker of *Close Encounters* and *E.T.* For all the novel's ostensible documentary harshness and sparse plotting, it contains enough outrageous coincidences and unexpected lineages and legacies to satisfy a Dickensian melodrama. Fresh from the Victoriana of *The Young Sherlock Holmes*, which he produced, Spielberg probably relished that aspect of the novel. In the movie, it is further underlined by early scenes in which, as part of their shared education, Celie and Nettie read and discuss Dickens's *Oliver Twist* – like *The Color Purple*, a novel of coincidence and social and sexual cruelty in which the sufferings of the victimized main character will eventually and miraculously be redeemed. *Oliver Twist* was made into a memorable film in 1948 by David Lean, one of Spielberg's favorite directors who seems to have been one of the major cinematic influences on Spielberg's film.

Undoubtedly, however, the single element in the story which reminds one most of Spielberg and makes it a less surprising subject for him to film than it immediately appears is the situation and character of Celie (Whoopi Goldberg). She has the loneliness of the boy in *E.T.* and is assailed by family storms and frictions like the mother in *Something Evil*, which she barely understands but ultimately has the inner

Below: Spielberg directs Whoopi Goldberg in *The Color Purple*. Her radiant performance secured an Oscar nomination.

power to resist. Above all, like many of Spielberg's most beloved characters, she is basically an innocent. Although sexually assaulted by the man she calls her father, brutally treated by her unloving husband and separated from her sister, her soul seems relatively unscathed: she is neither embittered nor degraded. She accepts her lot with a restrained, puzzled resignation rather than snarls resentfully against it. For a long time in the movie – this is part of her tragedy, as well as the reason she can survive – there is only a shadowy sense that she should expect, and richly deserves, something better. Even the crude, loveless sexuality of her marriage is adjusted to as the inevitable order of things: indeed, at one stage, Celie says she looks on the sexual act as being as functional as going to the toilet. According to her singer friend, Shug Avery (Margaret Avery), this means that Celie is 'still a virgin.'

Shug Avery is a crucial character in both novel and film. During the wedding night of Albert (Danny Glover) and Celie, Spielberg gives some visual prominence to the picture of Shug on the sideboard. She is, we discover, the love of Albert's life, the woman with whom he wished above all to share his bed; and, in the absence of Nettie, she will also become the love of Celie's, representing a healing feminine softness amid the brutish masculinity by which Celie has been surrounded. Shug is also a free spirit, a liberated woman who will stand as a defiant contrast to Celie's pensive passivity. Shug's influence will stiffen Celie's resolve. Celie says 'I don't know how to fight. All I know how to do is to stay alive.' Like the novel, the film is about the difference between merely existing and being fully alive. Shug Avery slowly shows Celie how to fight back.

Spielberg has been criticized for underplaying the importance of the lesbian relationship between Celie and Shug, which is made more explicit in the novel. It might be that he was not altogether convinced by it. It fits the importance the novel attaches to the theme of love and support between women, but is it psychologically convincing that someone as dynamic as Shug Avery would have been sexually attracted to someone as demure as Celie? In any case, Spielberg felt that it was not something he needed to emphasize: a kiss, an embrace, in a movie, he said, could serve as the equivalent of pages of exposition in a novel.

Right: Akosua Busia (right) as Nettie and Desreta Jackson as young Celie in *The Color Purple*.

Overleaf: Celie is determined to learn from her sister Nettie in *The Color Purple*.

Above: Whoopi Goldberg as the downtrodden Celie.

Left: When Nettie (left) rejects the advances of Celie's husband (Danny Glover), he throws her out of the house.

In fact, in the film, the love scene between Celie and Shug is exquisitely handled. It is preceded by a superb scene at Harpo's jukejoint, full of the most delicate shifts of mood in all the main characters, and in which Shug has serenaded Celie, half seriously, half ironically, with the song 'Miss Celie's Blues' – in effect, the first gift bestowed on Celie in her entire life. In the following scene, Shug draws attention to a noticeable characteristic of Celie's: her instinctive way of instantly covering up a smile with her hand. It is a gesture which says a lot about Celie's sense of oppression (not being allowed openly to laugh) but also about a concealed gaiety and humor beneath the surface of her quiet reticence. (Her action of secretly spitting in the drink of Albert's father has been another example of that: the suggestion of a covert rebelliousness in Celie that might one day surface and explode.) Now Shug encourages Celie to don her red gown and look at herself in the mirror. 'See? You got a beautiful smile, Miss Celie.' It is one of the loveliest moments in Spielberg's work, a sudden irradiation of happiness, a moment when a life of self-effacement is momentarily, magically transformed into a sign of self-recognition. When Celie discloses that her husband 'beats me for not being you,' Shug's sympathy blossoms into the tenderest of love scenes, Spielberg's camera delicately following the movement of Celie's hand as, in wonderment, she embraces Shug and discovers the touch of love.

It is Shug who discovers that Nettie (Akosua Busia) has been writing letters to Celie for years and that Albert has been hiding them. It turns out that Nettie has accompanied her adopted family (including Celie's children) to Africa and her letters are full of her African experience. Because of budgetary limitations, the African scenes had to be filmed in Carolina. Many critics derided the seeming phoniness of these scenes, particularly in comparison with the African footage of Sydney Pollack's *Out of Africa* (1985), which opened at roughly the same time as *The Color Purple* and was to prove its major Oscar rival.

However, it is possible to argue that realism was not Spielberg's primary purpose in the African scenes, and that his intentions here were different from Alice Walker's. In the novel, the African episodes seem designed to widen the thematic perspective from a consideration of Celie's specific suffering to a broader historical analysis of the mistreatment of black people. Equally significantly, they broaden the consciousness of the novel from the inevitably limited viewpoint of Celie to the more sophisticated, educated and wide-ranging perceptions of Nettie. In the film, Spielberg clearly wants to retain Celie as the center of the film's consciousness, its heart. If the African scenes in the film look inauthentic, they are not meant to represent Nettie's experience so much as Celie's *imagination* of that experience, triggered by her reading of Nettie's letters but conditioned by her limited perceptions.

On the whole, the African scenes are given less emphasis in the movie than in the novel. They explain where Nettie has been and her life with Celie's children. They provide a colorful, often ironic parallel to the events in America, as in the scene when an African sacrificial ceremony is crosscut with a tense episode where Celie, preparing to shave her husband, finds similarly primitive feelings stirring in her heart and bubbling toward a possibly murderous hatred for his part in separating her from her sister. Such imperious crosscutting, mystically forging a link between quite disparate events, already implies that the separation of distance between the two sisters will eventually be annihilated and they will finally be united in body as well as spirit.

The movie quotes the passage in the novel where Celie's daughter compares the refusal of the Olinka tribe to educate girls with 'white people at home who don't want colored people to learn.' One of the functions of the African scenes is to draw a parallel between the way whites subjugate blacks with the way men oppress women. The movie not only honors that theme in the novel: in some ways, it intensifies it. In the novel, Celie's husband will discover that 'meanness kills,' will repent of his past behavior, and is with Celie when she is reunited with her sister and her children. In the movie, Albert's transformation is a little more qualified. He does assist in the reunion between sisters, but the visual arrangement of the final scene suggests that he does it more out of a belated desire to regain the love and respect of Shug than to receive the forgiveness of Celie. Our final view of him is of a lonely, ghostly figure, excluded from the joyous circle, destroyed by a hopeless love, belatedly and vainly aware of what he has lost in his own family.

The movie's harsh treatment of Albert should caution one against assuming too quickly that Spielberg has sentimentalized the novel. There are important differences, of course. The movie is, one feels, more about individual resilience than feminist or racial politics. At the same time, it is no betrayal or crude simplification of the original novel. The visual style might be lusher and more polished than suggested by the novel's expressively choppy, colloquial prose, but it also has a kind of primitive directness that does effectively mirror the novel's style. The

Right: Celie in church. Whoopi Goldberg's meek, hesitant look epitomizes the character's timid self-effacement.

Above: Harpo (Willard Pugh) marries Sofia (Oprah Winfrey). Winfrey's performance won her an Oscar nomination.

tightening of the novel's discursiveness into a compact, compelling film narrative is a tribute to Menno Meyjes's skilful adaptation and to Spielberg's story-telling powers. There are some eloquent images: the idealized opening shot of two sisters playing and clapping in a field of purple flowers, which establishes the emotional frame of the film and which will be recalled at the end; the brief image of a bloodprint on the boundary stone of her new home after Celie has been attacked by Albert's son, Harpo (a portent of Celie's future suffering, a symbol of her husband's stony indifference); a shot of the empty mailbox which prefaces the scene of Shug's first arrival at Celie's home on a stormy night (an implication that Shug will fill the gap left in Celie's life by Nettie's absence and silence). This is a movie of consummate craftsmanship, in which every scene has been visually thought through.

One feels that the novel has three inspiriting influences behind it: the epistolary novel; the vernacular prose of Twain and Faulkner; and, according to Alice Walker herself, the stories told to her by her mother, in which she absorbed not only the content but something of the urgent manner in which she spoke of her memories and experience. This latter point probably underlines a major difference in feeling between novel and film; Alice Walker is drawing partly on her own history to tell the story, whereas Spielberg is drawing (however sympathetically) on film history. Inevitably, in consequence, the movie seems a little more calculated and detached, though palpably sincere.

Spielberg's cinematic mentors for *The Color Purple* seem to have been D W Griffith, John Ford and David Lean. One recognizes the Griffith influence in the unashamed emotion and the attention to tremulous female suffering. John Ford is recalled in the way Spielberg composes his scenes on the family porch, and in the film's occasional use of rough slapstick for comic relief. There is probably more humor in the movie than in the novel, though the fun always has a double-edge. Celie's anticipation of Albert's confusion when he is dressing to meet Shug, calmly handing him his shoes, cufflinks and tie he has forgotten, is funny but also a sharp cameo of the invisible, obedient wife in the background, more servant than partner. The belligerence of Harpo's wife, Sofia (Oprah Winfrey), is funny when it happens in Harpo's jukejoint but not at all funny when she strikes back later on being harassed by the (white) mayor and his wife. Sofia will come to exemplify the dangers, as well as the joys, of a black woman in that community fighting against her fate.

The greatest influence on Spielberg's direction of *The Color Purple* is surely David Lean. The film has the authoritative expansiveness of a Lean epic like *Lawrence of Arabia* (1962) and *Dr Zhivago* (1965) and the emotional impact of Lean's Dickensian adaptations, *Great Expectations* (1946) and *Oliver Twist*. It recalls Lean also in tiny visual details, like Celie's first glimpse of Albert through a patch of condensation on the window, or her trailing behind her mother's hearse – both shots which recall similar compositions in *Dr Zhivago*. Most noticeable is Spielberg's brilliant use of visual and aural transitions between scenes, which is an aspect of Lean's art which Spielberg especially admires. For example, the soundmatch of clapping hands and horses' hooves signals a cut from a scene between Celie and Nettie which emphasize their togetherness to one that will drive them apart, as Albert pursues Nettie on horseback prior to his attempted seduction and failed rape. Such transitions hustle the narrative forward and testify to the care of the film's structure and the precision of Michael Kahn's editing.

Technically, *The Color Purple* is a considerable achievement. There are at least three great set-pieces: the jukejoint scene with Shug and Celie; a dazzling dinner table scene, where Celie finally turns on Albert and where gradually, male supremacy around the table is triumphantly and joyously vanquished by the other women; and a reconciliation scene between Shug and her preacher father, which has no equivalent in the novel and which is done entirely through music and montage, as New Orleans jazz harmonizes gradually with Negro gospel in a hymn of reconciliation. Allen Daviau's photography is richly textured; Quincy Jones's music is unashamedly sentimental; and the set design and decoration of J. Michael Riva, Linda de Scenna, Virginia Randolph and Robert Welch deserving of the highest praise.

There is no question that the technicians have given Spielberg what he wanted: the only question is whether this style is appropriate for this subject or whether something a little more raw, less technically finished, might have been more suitable for the texture of the novel's emotions. On the other hand, a tougher, tetchier movie might have been seen by and touched the feelings of infinitely fewer people. Spielberg's tactic of making a kind of *Gone With the Wind* for a new age has been accomplished with a minimum of compromise and distortion. He is assisted by performances from Whoopi Goldberg, Margaret Avery, Oprah Winfrey,

Above: Sofia's troubles begin when she repudiates the attentions of the Mayor's wife (Dana Ivey, left) and refuses to apologise to the Mayor (Phillip Stone, center).

Danny Glover and the whole supporting cast which it is difficult to imagine being bettered. Goldberg's performance, in particular, is a remarkably resourceful and poignant piece of screen acting.

The Color Purple ran into a storm of controversy almost as soon as it opened. It was first attacked for implicit racism for its depiction of Negro males as 'cruel bullies': if this is a fault of the film, it is one it shares with the novel. (In its defense, a number of people claimed that the characterization in novel and film was basically true to many people's experience: it is clear also in the movie that black men have probably been conditioned to behave in that way because of their own treatment at the hands of whites.) Ironically, when its three main female performers were passed over for Oscars, the Hollywood Academy was accused of racial discrimination against the film by the Beverley Hills branch of the NACP (National Association of Colored People).

It was the Oscar controversy over *The Color Purple* which particularly hit the headlines. The film was nominated for 11 Oscars, but Spielberg was not nominated as best director, the first time for over 40 years that a movie with 10 or

Below: Mister (Danny Glover) in bed with Shug Avery (Margaret Avery), the woman he loves but whom his father forbade him to marry.

Above: Shug serenades Celie with 'Miss Celie's Blues.'

more nominations had not been nominated for a directing Oscar. The production company, Warners, took the unusual step of issuing a statement thanking the Academy for the nominations but castigating it for Spielberg's omission: 'The company is shocked and dismayed that the movie's primary creative force – Steven Spielberg – was not recognized.' Spielberg's disappointment was somewhat allayed by two alternative, prestigious awards around the Oscar time: the best director award from the Directors Guild of America, and the award of the Fellowship of the British Film Institute. But, to rub salt into the wounds, *The Color Purple* was to win no Oscars at all, while its chief rival *Out of Africa* was to win seven.

Above left: Celie and Shug develop a loving friendship, an expression of female solidarity in a harsh masculine world.

Left: With the help of Shug, Celie discovers Nettie's letters, which Mister has concealed from her for several years.

Right: Spielberg converses with his co-producer on *The Color Purple*, Frank Marshall (right).

Above: Reverend Samuel (Carl Anderson) embraces his wife (Susan Beaubian) as soldiers force them to leave their African village. A tense Nettie (Akosua Brusia, left) looks on during one of the African sequences in *The Color Purple*.

Left: Neither Celie nor Mister is pleased when Shug returns with a new husband, Grady (Bennet Guillory, right).

Below: Celie at last tells Mister what she thinks of him and triumphantly leaves him to start a better life with Shug.

gun-battle in the streets of Shanghai and an air-raid on the internment camp are two of the most thrilling action set-pieces of recent cinema. Elsewhere he scrupulously reproduces vivid images from the novel: the beggar at the gate of Jim's home, an omen of the penury the family is shortly to face; the footprints in the talcum powder on the bedroom floor, which alert Jim to the fact that his mother has been captured. Most memorable of all is the white light that suddenly suffuses (like 'a second sun') the deserted Xanadu-like stadium at which Jim and his fellow prisoners are required to rest. It is the atomic bomb dropping on Hiroshima, signifying the end of the war, and maybe the end of God's universe.

Spielberg's visual craftsmanship is as consummate as ever. There are many visual motifs that are unobtrusive and natural in context but subtly bind the structure together: recurrent images of flames, to suggest Jim's whole childhood as a baptism of fire; shots through windows and veils that drape a cloak of protective innocence over Jim's premature confrontation with death and sex; two moments when Jim is stopped dead in his tracks, the first to mark his first real involvement in the war, the second to mark its end. The technical excellence of Allen Daviau's photography, Michael Kahn's editing and Norman Reynolds' production design are, of course, indispensable to the realization of Spielberg's vision.

The film has been very well cast. John Malkovich's Basie has a cheeky competitiveness but also the ruthless streak of the survivor that can be dangerous to anyone in its path. Basie is an unsettling mixture of charisma and corruptions: Malkovich blends the ingredients astutely. Equally well-judged performances come from Nigel Havers as Dr Rawlins, having just the right quality of fussy, pompous decency that gets on Jim's nerves; and from Miranda Richardson as the enigmatic Mrs Victor, epitomizing Ballard's conception of the character as 'a handsome if frayed blonde' whose 'nerves were always stretched.'

If ultimately the film gives a sense of greatness not quite achieved, the reason perhaps is that the film, in striving so hard to be an epic, rather glosses over the original's introspective power. Tom Stoppard's screenplay is an elegant exercise in tasteful transposition, but it lacks the imaginative touches that distinguish the adaptation of *The Color Purple*. John Williams's score has its haunting and awesome moments, but Williams is not as good as Jerry Goldsmith at getting under the skin of a complex drama: his music here offers a moving but rather generalized emo-tional display. There is sometimes a similar sense of dramatic inflation about Spielberg's direction, as in the boy's reaction to the death of the Kamikaze pilot. It is great cinema, but does it ring emotionally true? It is instructive here to compare *Empire of the Sun* with Elem Klimov's Soviet film, *Come and See* (1985), which also details the horrors of war as seen through the eyes of a child. They are both the work of exceptional cineastes, but the emotional atmosphere is different – the difference between the work of a man who knows war basically through war movies, and one whose country's wartime suffering has indelibly scorched itself on his consciousness. Nevertheless, *Empire of the Sun* still succeeds as a potent picture of childhood *in extremis*.

What of the future? One of the most noticeable aspects of Spielberg's recent development has been the widening stylistic gap between the movies he produces – as he puts it, movies he would like to see but not direct – and the movies he personally makes. In 1986, the new production included Barry Levinson's *Young Sherlock Holmes*, Richard Benjamin's *The Money Pit* and the Don Bluth cartoon, *An American Tail*. More recently, we have had Joe Dante's *Innerspace* (1987), William Dear's *Bigfoot and the Hendersons* (1987), Matthew Robbins's *Batteries Not*